PASTOR—

This gift book is in appreciation for your fellowship in the World Literature Crusade Radio Missionary Convention.

Oswald J. Smith

THE BATTLE FOR TRUTH

THE BATTLE FOR TRUTH

BY

OSWALD J. SMITH, Litt.D.

(Pastor of The Peoples Church, Toronto)

Foreword by

Dr. NATHAN R. WOOD

(Formerly President, Gordon College, Boston)

London

MARSHALL, MORGAN & SCOTT

Edinburgh

LONDON
MARSHALL, MORGAN AND SCOTT, LTD.
1-5 PORTPOOL LANE
HOLBORN, E.C.1

AUSTRALIA
117-119 BURWOOD ROAD
MELBOURNE, E.13

SOUTH AFRICA
P.O. BOX 1720, STURK'S BUILDINGS
CAPE TOWN

CANADA
EVANGELICAL PUBLISHERS
241 YONGE STREET
TORONTO

THE PEOPLES PRESS
100 BLOOR STREET EAST
TORONTO

U.S.A.
WORLD LITERATURE CRUSADE PRESS
BOX 1313, STUDIO CITY
CALIFORNIA

First published 1953
Second impression 1954
Third impression 1956
Fourth impression 1957
Fifth impression 1961

MADE AND PRINTED IN GREAT BRITAIN BY PURNELL AND SONS, LTD.
PAULTON (SOMERSET) AND LONDON

FOREWORD

HAVE YOU heard Oswald Smith? Have you felt the prophetic fire, the apostolic fervour, of his messages? An electric current of life runs through them. They go straight to the point. Some of them are a chain of unbroken logic, but, like Finney's reasoning sermons, they are "chain lightning".

We should be glad when Oswald Smith puts some of those discourses into a book. For something of the passion, the earnestness, the loving purpose, somehow conveys itself in print. You realize, too, as you read, what the public delivery did not give you time to pause and grasp, that the English style of the discourses is unusually fine. It is a literary as well as a spoken style.

It is always clear and vivid. You never question what a sentence means. Short, direct sentences, yet never staccato, and constantly varied in rhythm, and in appeal to mind and heart, show that the speaker and writer knows this secret of English style. It is one reason for the great reading audience of his books. And it is right to call his readers an "audience", for you somehow hear as well as read with the book before you.

A yet greater secret is the power of the Spirit speaking through these human words. And an equally great reason is the emphasis on Christ rather than the speaker in human lives.

The messages in this book cover a wide range. They are varied, practical and biblical, reflecting the interests of a preacher who is at once an evangelist, the pastor of a great church, and a missionary administrator. To

FOREWORD

Boston readers they bring back vividly the speaker's wonderful campaign in the Park Street Church and Gordon College, and his notable missionary conference a few months later.

A hand-book of many subjects, a heart-to-heart talk on perplexing questions, an exposition of many Scripture passages, a trumpet warning in a darkening day, an eloquent heralding of Christ, a vision of the world to be, all in one book! May it be blessed, as *The Man God Uses, The Revival We Need* and other Spirit-filled utterances of the lips and pen of this preacher of Christ have been blessed and used in countless lives!

N. R. WOOD

Formerly President
Gordon College, Boston

CONTENTS

THEN JESUS CAME

Oswald J. Smith

Homer Rodeheaver

1. One sat a-lone be-side the high-way beg-ging, His eyes were blind, the
2. From home and friends the e-vil spir-its drove him, A-mong the tombs he
3. "Un-clean! un-clean!" the le-per cried in tor-ment, The deaf, the dumb, in
4. Their hearts were sad as in the tomb they laid him, For death had come and
5. So men to-day have found the Sav-iour a-ble, They could not con-quer

light he could not see; He clutched his rags and shiv-ered in the shad-ows,
dwelt in mis-er-y; He cut him-self as de-mon pow'rs pos-sessed him,
help-less-ness stood near; The fe-ver raged, dis-ease had gripped its vic-tim,
tak-en him a-way; Their night was dark and bit-ter tears were fall-ing,
pas-sion, lust and sin; Their bro-ken hearts had left them sad and lone-ly,

REFRAIN

Then Je-sus came and bade his dark-ness flee.
Then Je-sus came and set' the cap-tive free.
Then Je-sus came and cast out ev-'ry fear.
Then Je-sus came and night was turned to day.
Then Je-sus came and dwelt, Him-self, with-in.

When Je-sus comes the

tempt-er's pow'r is bro-ken; When Je-sus comes the tears are wiped a-way. He takes the

gloom and fills the life with glo-ry, For all is changed when Je-sus comes to stay.

CHAPTER I

TURN WITH me, if you will, to the Gospel according to Matthew, the thirteenth chapter, verses forty-one and forty-two: "The Son of man shall send forth his angels, and they shall gather out of his kingdom all things that offend, and them which do iniquity; and shall cast them into a furnace of fire: there shall be wailing and gnashing of teeth."

When I was a boy I saw a sight that I never can forget—a man carried out of his house in a sheet, in the dead of night. I was watching from an upper window and I was told that the man had gone insane and that he was being taken to a lunatic asylum. Never will I forget the impression it made upon me. I can still remember it.

It may be that there are those in this audience who have had loved ones put away in an asylum, and if so then you know something about it. Death would have been preferable. Perhaps even now you are thinking of a dear one who will have to spend the remainder of his days in such an institution.

We must have asylums to safeguard society. The sane and the insane cannot mix. They simply must be kept apart. For the sake and safety of the sane the insane must be put away.

Now God has an asylum. He, too, knows that the sane and the insane could never be happy together, and so in His asylum—which, by the way, was never prepared for man—the insane will one day have to be put. His asylum was made for the devil and his angels; but since it is the only one He has, therefore the spiritually insane have to be sent to it.

Have you ever visited an asylum? Have you ever seen the insane? I have. One sits thinking, thinking. Another continually weeps. Others wail aloud and gnash their teeth. Their brains have been deranged. They are not themselves. Hence they suffer, suffer in an indescribable way, and there is very little that can be done for them.

God's asylum is called Gehenna, and it is mentioned twelve times in the New Testament Scriptures: eleven times by Christ Himself and once by James. John calls it the Lake of Fire and the Second Death. I have called it the Madhouse of the Universe.

This asylum is a place of conscious suffering. Such words as fire, weeping, wailing, the gnashing of teeth, are used to describe it. Fire burns. People do not weep when they are happy, nor do they wail unless they are miserable. When they gnash their teeth they must be suffering real pain.

So terrible is it that Jesus recommended the loss of hand, foot and eye in preference to being consigned to it.

God Does Not Want You to Go There

Let me make it clear, however, that God does not want you to go there.

First of all, it is not His will that *any* should perish. He Himself says so. "Not willing that any should perish" (2 Pet. iii. 9). Hence if you perish and have to be consigned to the asylum prepared for the devil and his angels it will be your own fault. It is not the will of God.

In the second place, God has provided deliverance for you. He has redeemed all mankind. Salvation may be yours; there is no reason, then, why you should ever be consigned to the Madhouse of the Universe. "Christ . . .

is the propitiation for . . . the sins of the whole world" (1 John ii. 12).

In the third place, let me point out that He urges you to be saved. "Be ye reconciled to God" (2 Cor. v. 20). Again and again throughout the Scriptures He pleads with you to be reconciled. Hence it is not His plan to put you in the asylum that was never prepared for you, but if you refuse to be saved He has no alternative but to send you there.

Who Are the Insane?

Now who are the insane? That is the important question; and I want to make five suggestions, if I may, so that you can decide whether or not *you* are insane.

First of all, the man is insane who prepares for the present and not for the future.

You remember the rich fool. He stored up his grain in his barns; he made an abundant provision for the present; he felt satisfied that he had all that he needed for the rest of his life, and yet God pronounced him a fool; God called him a lunatic, and told him that that very night his soul would be required of him. Why was he insane? Not because he was wealthy, not because he had worked hard, not because he had saved; but because he had made no preparation for the future. The preparation he made was for the present. He gave no thought to his soul. His only thought was for his body. Hence God pronounced him a lunatic. That man was headed for the asylum—the Madhouse of the Universe.

Second, the man is insane who thinks he can sin and get away with it.

God has said, "Be sure your sin will find you out." No man can sin and escape punishment. "The soul that sinneth, it shall die." That is what God says. "The wages of sin is death." This again is God's pronouncement. Hence for a man to think that he can go on sinning and get away with it at last is insanity in itself. That man is a lunatic and is headed for the Madhouse of the Universe. Are you that man? I leave you to answer the question.

Third, the man is insane who rejects God's plan and manufactures one of his own.

God has provided for man's salvation. There is no other way of escape. God gave His Son to die on Calvary's cross and to bear your sins in order that you might not have to bear them. If you reject God's plan and manufacture one of your own, whether it be one of works or religion, or anything else, you are most assuredly insane. Why not accept the God-provided plan? Why try to invent one of your own?

Do you really think that your plan is better than God's? Have you an idea that you can become so religious that you can escape God's asylum? Or do you think that by living a good life you can become sane and thus never have to be consigned to the Madhouse of the Universe? Away with such a thought! God is not going to allow you to substitute your plan for His. There is no other way. You must come through Christ as a poor, helpless, hell-deserving sinner, or not at all.

Fourth, the man is insane who puts off his salvation until his death-bed.

I know the thief was saved on the cross just before he died, but may I point out that the other thief was not? Therefore you are taking a terrible chance. I do not believe the thief ever had another chance. Probably the first time he met the Lord Jesus Christ was when he saw Him hanging by his side on the accursed tree. But you have heard the message again and again. Time after time God's servants have pleaded with you to be reconciled to God and yet you have gone on in your rebellion and rejection, refusing God's offer of mercy.

You have an idea that you can accept Jesus Christ on your death-bed. I would not take that chance for all the world. It has been my privilege to visit a great many of my parishioners who have passed on into the other life, and I want to bear testimony to the fact that in most cases they were far too weak at the end to even think about making a decision for the Lord Jesus Christ. Many who are dying are kept under drugs; their minds are confused; they cannot think aright. How, then, can they make such a momentous decision?

My friend, any moment you may be cut off. Little did the rich fool think that he would be called to an account that very night. On every side we are surrounded by accidents. In this mechanized world the newspaper is simply filled with reports of accidental deaths. Are you going to take a chance? You are insane if you do; and if you should be cut off without warning, remember—you will go to the Madhouse of the Universe.

These, then, are the men and the women who are insane; and if they are insane now, and if they die in their insanity, what can God do but assign them to His asylum, where all must go who are spiritually insane? It would be impossible for God to allow them to associate with those who are spiritually sane. They would have nothing in common with them. Hence he has to separate them, and the only plan He has is to send them to Gehenna, the place we call hell, where the devil and his angels are to be consigned, there to be eternally separated from those who have accepted Jesus Christ and are therefore sane in the sight of God.

Jesus speaks of the tares being gathered and burned in the fire, and then He says, "So shall it be in the end of this world", or, as it is in the original, "at the end of this age". He Himself will send forth His angels. They are the only ones who can distinguish the sane from the insane. First of all they will gather out of His Kingdom all that offend and those who practise iniquity. They will be cast into a furnace of fire, namely, God's asylum, the Madhouse of the Universe, and there, the Lord says, "there shall be wailing and gnashing of teeth".

After that He tells us about the sane, and He calls the sane the righteous. He says that they are to shine forth as the sun in the Kingdom of their Father. The great division has taken place. The insane have been separated from the sane, and now those, by God pronounced sane, are to dwell together, shining as the sun through all the countless ages of eternity.

My friend, to which group do you belong? Are you sane or insane? Will you spend your eternity with the sane in the Kingdom of God, or will you be consigned to the Madhouse of the Universe?

They Were Insane

Thomas Paine was insane. He would call out during his paroxysms of distress, without intermission, "O Lord, help me! God, help me! Jesus Christ, help me! O Lord, help me!" etc., repeating the same expressions without the least variations, in a tone that would alarm the house. That is a picture of an insane man. He was insane before he died, hence he has gone to the place of the insane.

Voltaire was insane. For three months remorse, reproach and blasphemy accompanied and characterized the long agony of the dying atheist. His death, the most terrible that is ever recorded to a stricken and impious man, will not be denied even by his companions in impiety. Rage succeeded to fury, and fury to rage again. The conspirators could hear him, the prey of anguish and dread,

alternately supplicating or blaspheming that God whom
he had conspired against; and in plaintive accents would
he cry out, "O Christ! O Jesus Christ!" and then com-
plain that he was abandoned by God and man. His physicians, thunder-struck, retired, declaring the death of the
impious man to be terrible indeed. These were the cries of
insanity. Voltaire spent his life as an insane man and
then went to the Madhouse of the Universe.

Francis Newport was also insane. At the end of his life
he wrote: "How idle is it to bid the fire not to burn when
fuel is administered, and to command the sea to be smooth
in the midst of a storm! Such is my case. Whither am
I going? Damned and lost forever." His voice failed
and he began to struggle and gasp for breath; which,
having recovered, with a groan dreadful and horrid,
as if it had been more than human, cried out, "Oh, the
insufferable pangs of hell and damnation!" and then
expired.

I once heard of a dying universalist who was most certainly insane. His exclamation was, "I have despised
mercy! I have scoffed at God! I have refused Christ!
My day has gone by! I am lost! I am lost! Oh, fool!
fool! I have been a fool all my days!" He, too, was
bound for the Madhouse of the Universe.

When Jennie Gordon was dying she cried, "The fiends,
they come; Oh, save me! They drag me down! Lost!
Lost! Lost! Bind me, ye chains of darkness! Oh that I
might cease to be, but still exist." These, again, are the
exclamations and ravings of the insane. Her soul was
doomed, and she, too, was on her way to the Madhouse
of the Universe.

There was once a young girl who wanted to be saved,
but her father said, "If my daughter goes to that altar I
will wade in blood to take her out of there." She did not
go. Later she became seriously ill and God started to deal

with her. Suddenly she cried aloud, "My doom is sealed forever." Then, "What time is it?" Her father told her that it was four o'clock. "Just think," she said, "I am going where there is no time." A moment later she spoke again. "Father," she cried, "get me a drink from the old well, for I am going where there is no water."

A little later she spoke once more. "Father," she said, "put your arms under me and pull me up. My feet are on fire. My feet are slipping. Take my feet out of the fire." After thus agonizing, she again requested, "Bring your daughter another drink of water." He started to get it, but before he got back his beautiful daughter had gone into eternity.

Insane she lived. Insane she died. And in her spiritual insanity she went where thousands, yea hundreds of thousands, of others are doomed to go—she went to the Madhouse of the Universe.

My friends, I could go on. The whole world is insane and is bound for the Madhouse of the Universe. Only those who open their hearts to the Lord Jesus Christ and accept Him as a personal Saviour ever become sane. It is for you to decide your own destiny. Are you going to spend it with the sane or with the insane, with the children of God or with the children of Satan, saved or lost, in Heaven above or in the Madhouse of the Universe? It is for you to say.

If you refuse, you are insane and you do not want to become sane. You are determined to spend your eternity in the Madhouse of the Universe rather than in the Paradise of God. You prefer the company of the insane to the company of the sane. What a choice!

And yet the insane may become sane. Lunatics can be restored to their right minds. God can do for the spiritually insane what no doctor can do for the mentally insane. But not against your will. You must co-operate with Him by choosing Jesus Christ, His Son, as your Saviour.

How must I plead with you? What more can I say? Will you love your sin and go to hell, or leave your sin and go to heaven? "Turn ye, oh, turn ye, for why will ye die?" Choose now. Don't put it off. "Seek ye the Lord while he may be found." Make certain that you do not spend your eternity in the Madhouse of the Universe.

Note—This chapter was the prize-winning sermon in The Sword of the Lord Contest.

CHAPTER II

THE GREATEST VERSE IN THE BIBLE

THIS BOOK I hold in my hand is the Bible. It is the greatest book in the world. No man is educated until he knows the Bible. I have read it every day of my life for over forty years, and I am going to read it every day until I see my Saviour face to face. I would urge you to do the same.

Many years ago an African chief visited Queen Victoria in England. When he was leaving he asked her a question. "Your Majesty," he inquired, "what is the secret of England's greatness?" "The Bible," was the immediate response of the Queen.

"Righteousness exalteth a nation, but sin is a reproach to any people," declares the Word of God. The nation that turns from the Bible is doomed. It was the Reformation that made Germany the leading nation of Europe, and the Reformation was based on the Bible; and when Germany denied the authority of the Bible she perished. When France substituted sin for righteousness she was lost. "Be not deceived; God is not mocked: for whatsoever a man soweth, that shall he also reap" (Gal. vi. 7). And what is true of nations is also true of individuals.

This Book means more to me than any other book in the world. It is my meat and my drink. The more I study it, the more I love it. There is no other like it. It is God's Book. When I read it God speaks to me. I hear His voice. By it men are saved. By it men live. And by it men are going to be judged. It is our one and only authority. This

Book will keep you from sin, or sin will keep you from this Book.

Now the greatest book in the Bible is the Gospel of John. And the greatest chapter in John's Gospel is the third. The greatest verse in the third chapter is the sixteenth. And this is what it says: "For God so loved the world, that he gave his only begotten Son, that whosoever believeth in him should not perish, but have everlasting life."

This, my friends, is the heart of the Gospel. More souls have been saved through John iii. 16 than through any other verse. It is the best-known verse in the Bible and it has been translated into more languages than any other. It is the greatest statement concerning the love of God on record. Moreover, it is God's Word.

About a thousand years ago now a Jewish song-writer, Meir Ben-Isaac Nehoric, wrote a stanza about the love of God, which was later published in *A Book of Jewish Thoughts*, compiled by Joseph Herman Hertz, Chief Rabbi of the British Empire. But no one ever heard of it until one day it was found pencilled on the wall of an insane asylum by an inmate who had died. How he had found it no one will ever know. In my mind it is the greatest poem on the love of God ever written. Here it is:

> *Could we with ink the ocean fill,*
> *   And were the skies of parchment made;*
> *Were ev'ry stalk on earth a quill,*
> *   And ev'ry man a scribe by trade;*
> *To write the love of God above*
> *   Would drain the ocean dry;*
> *Nor could the scroll contain the whole,*
> *   Though stretched from sky to sky.*

In John iii. 16, we have four tremendous statements regarding the love of God.

First—"For God so loved the world"

"For *God* so loved . . ." Salvation starts with God. You had nothing to do with it. Before you were born God provided it for you. Don't think you can discover God. You never can. God is revealed, not discovered. He took the first step.

"For God *so* loved . . ." That little word "so" speaks volumes. It explains all that follows, all that Christ endured for you, all that God suffered when He gave Christ. All He saves you from and all that He provides for you is because He *so* loved you.

"For God so *loved* . . ." The gods of the heathen are gods of hate and fear. Our God is a God of love. The heathen are afraid of their gods. We love our God. Their gods are gods of judgment, power and cruelty, bent on doing them injury. Our God is a God of judgment and power also, but first and foremost He is a God of love, seeking to do us good.

God does not love man's sin, but He loves man. You do not love your child's disease but you love your child. Such love as God's is unfathomable. It is a love that cannot be understood, but a love that is real nevertheless. I want you, my friend, to know that God loves you. He loves you no matter what you have done, no matter how great your sin, and He always will love you in spite of your attitude towards Him.

"For God so loved the *world* . . ." That is what makes it impossible for the human mind to comprehend the love of God. The world is made up of rebels, men who have turned their backs on God. Yet, in spite of their rebellion, God loved them. The Bible says that "God commendeth His love towards us in that while we were yet sinners, Christ died for us"; and again it says, "Christ died for the ungodly." God loved not alone the good but the bad. When Jesus was being nailed to the cross He prayed, "Father, forgive them, for they know not what they do." Such love is not human. It is divine. In spite of your enmity, God loves you. What marvellous, matchless love!

Had God wiped out the race as He destroyed the Antediluvians by the flood, and Sodom and Gomorrah by fire, we could have understood it, for that is what man would have done. We did not forgive the Nazi leaders of Germany and give them another chance; we executed them. Such is man's inhumanity to man. That is the way man acts. But not so God. His love forgives. God is merciful. He loves the unlovely, the rebellious and the sinful. Such love is supernatural. It is divine. For only God loves like that.

Had He loved only the lovely, the good and obedient, we could have understood it, for we love those who love us. We love our friends; that is human love. But God loves His enemies. He loves the disobedient and sinful. That love we cannot understand. It is beyond our comprehension.

The prodigal's father, you remember, loved his erring son, even though he disgraced him by his life of debauchery and sin. He was waiting with outstretched arms to receive him. "This my son was dead and is alive again," he cried. "He was lost, and is found" (Luke xv. 24). What a welcome! Such is the love of God.

Second—"That he gave his only begotten Son"

"For God so loved the world that He *gave* . . ." Love demands sacrifice. Love produces action. Love must demonstrate itself. That is true even of human love. God has proved His love by giving.

"For God so loved the world that he gave his only begotten *Son* . . ." He could have sent an angel or even an archangel, but he didn't. He sent His Son, His nearest and His dearest. Nothing could have demonstrated His love like the giving of His only begotten Son. A father will give everything he possesses before he will give his son.

Bear in mind, if you will, that God could have rescued His Son even from the cross, and yet He let Him suffer and never raised a hand to save Him. Would you have done that? Could you, as a father, have let your son suffer such excruciating agony, knowing full well that you had the power to rescue him, to save him from it all, and yet never make an effort to do anything? Impossible! There isn't a father in the world who could stand by and see wicked men drive cruel spikes into the hands and feet of his son and not make an effort to save him.

But God did. God allowed His Son to die when He could have rescued Him. That is what makes His love so wonderful. It is a love beyond human understanding. It is not human; it is divine. God's love is so great that He could allow His Son to suffer and die and make no effort to save Him, when He could have done so at any time. Such love, I say, is beyond human comprehension. He did it because of his love for you. To save you He had to let His Son die.

Isaac, you remember, was saved, for just as Abraham was about to slay him God cried out, "Abraham, Abraham. Lay not thine hand upon the lad" (Gen. xxii. 12). But when Jesus, in the agony of His soul, exclaimed, "My God, my God, why hast thou forsaken me?" (Matt. xxvii. 46), there was no voice that answered. God turned away His face and let Him die. To save you He had to sacrifice His Son. Oh, what love!

Third—"That whosoever believeth in him"

Now there are three great things in this statement expressed by three words.

First, *whosoever*. Here we have the universality of God's offer of salvation. It is for you, for me, or for anybody else. It takes in the yellow and the brown, the black and the white. It includes sinners of the deepest dye, as well as those who have lived moral and upright lives. It makes no difference what a man is or what he has done. He is included in God's *whosoever*.

Peter thought it was only for the Jews, and God had to give him a special vision before he would go to the Gentiles. God's love is universal, and so is His salvation. It is for Jew and Gentile alike.

I urge you, then, to come to Him. You need not fear, I do not care what you have done or who you are. God offers you salvation just like anybody else. Drunkards, harlots, liars, thieves, dope-fiends, blasphemers—all may come. God says, *whosoever*.

The second word is the word *believeth*. "Whosoever *believeth* in him." Faith connects the sinner with God. It simply means trusting Jesus Christ. In other words, you must lean your whole weight on Him. It is a word of action. It has nothing whatever to do with your intellect. It does not say that you must believe certain things about Jesus Christ. It says you must trust Him.

You must trust Him as you trust an elevator when you step into it; as you trust a boat when you go aboard; as you trust a street car when you enter it. Forget your intellect. Never mind what you believe or what you do not believe. Dare to venture all on Jesus Christ; that is trust. You have believed all your life, now you must act, and when you do you will be saved.

It is "not of works" (Eph. ii. 9). There is nothing you can do to merit it. All your prayers and fastings will not save you. All your church-going and religious practices will be unavailing. Penance, self-denial, bodily afflictions, pilgrimages—works of any kind—all, yea, all, will be ineffective. For you are saved, not by works, but by faith.

The third word is the word *him*, referring, of course, to the Lord Jesus Christ. "Whosoever believeth in him." Do not worry about your faith. It makes no difference whether you have much or little, nor what kind of faith it is. It may only be like a grain of mustard seed. Forget your faith. Think now of the object of your faith. Think of the One you are to trust. Put your faith in a person and let that person be the Lord Jesus Christ.

It is not your *faith* that saves you; it is Christ. Why, then, worry about your faith? Look to Jesus. Rely upon Him. He is the One who saves. Dare, then, to trust Him.

If you put your faith in the wrong person you will never be saved. If you put your faith in religion or in the church you will not be saved. If you put it in your good works, your morality, again, you will not be saved; but if you put it in Christ He will save you. "Believe on the *Lord Jesus Christ* and thou shalt be saved." He is your one and only hope. That is why God says, "Whosoever believeth in *him*."

Fourth—"Should not perish but have everlasting life"

There are two things here. First, we are saved from something—"should not perish". We are saved from death. Second, we are given something—"but have everlasting life". We are given life.

To perish means to die, and to die eternally means to be forever separated from God. That is spiritual death.

According to God's word, men are "dead in trespasses and in sins", and they have to be quickened into life. I am preaching now to dead men, to corpses, and Jesus says, "Ye shall die in your sins." In other words, unless you receive eternal life you will pass out of this life as you are, namely, "dead in trespasses and in sins".

Look at this fruit. See these vegetables. They all look good. But they are perishing. They are in a state of death. Soon they will become corrupt. Little by little they will rot away. As a matter of fact, they are dead already, for they have been severed from the tree and from the vine. So it is with you. Appearances do not matter. You are already dead; you are right now perishing. The lake of fire awaits you. Eternal death will be your doom. There is no hope; you cannot be saved— unless you are quickened into life, unless you are grafted into God.

Now God wants to save you from death, and so He offers you life, everlasting life. And I come to you today as His ambassador, with His message of life, eternal life. I offer you now God-life, uncreated life, the life of the ages. Will you have it? Do you want to remain in a state of death? Or do you want this glorious, indestructible life that God now offers you? It is for you to decide.

I cannot explain it. I do not understand it myself, but I know I have it. I have had it ever since I accepted Jesus Christ as my Saviour. I became a partaker of divine life and that life is mine today. I know where I am going. Death will not mean a plunge into the dark so far as I am concerned. "He loved me and gave himself for me." I accepted Him as my Saviour and now I have His life. Therefore, I will never perish, and no one will ever pluck me out of His hand. I am His and He is mine, and mine for all eternity.

This, my friend, is the love of God. Is it not wonderful?

What matchless grace! What a glorious revelation! How can you spurn it? How can you turn away? What will you say when you stand before Him? He can forgive anything. But to despise His love, to spurn His offer of mercy, to reject His only begotten Son—that is something that never can be forgiven.

I plead with you because God loves you. This one verse alone is sufficient to prove it. Herein is the Gospel. It is now for you to open your heart and receive the Lord Jesus Christ as your own personal Saviour. "For God so loved the world, that he gave his only begotten Son, that whosoever believeth in him should not perish, but have everlasting life."

"Can You Tell Me the Way to Heaven?"

Let me tell you a story. I read it in a tract. It is rather long, so I am going to condense it for you.

It was during the First World War. Shells were bursting all around. Presently there was a black cloud as pieces of shrapnel came whizzing past. Poor Bert fell like a log. Tiny Jim (6 ft. 3 ins.) jumped down beside him and then returned to his place in the trench.

Suddenly there was a startled cry, "Can you tell me the way to heaven?" Tiny jumped down again. "The way to heaven? I'm sorry, chum, I don't know the way, but I'll ask the other fellows."

He returned to the fire-step and walked along to the next man and asked him, but he did not know. So he went on to the man beyond him, but he did not know either. Jumping down, he walked around the trench into the next fire-bay, jumped up on the fire-step and inquired of the third man. Then he went from one to another until he had asked seven men the same question, but none of them knew the way to heaven.

Leaving that part of the trench, he went on to the next. His question was always the same, "Bert is dying. He wants to know the way to heaven. Can you tell him the way?" He had now asked sixteen men, but not one of them could answer his question.

Finally Tiny Jim reached a machine-gunner sitting alone with his gun, his eyes glued on the German lines. The gunner felt a thump on his back and then heard a voice shouting, "Gunner, there is a chap in our company who has been hit. He's dying and he wants to know the way to heaven. Can you tell him the way?"

The machine-gunner turned around and a smile lit up his face as he replied. "Yes," he said, "I know the way, but I cannot get along the trench. I dare not leave my gun. But wait." Thrusting his hand into his pocket he pulled out a little Testament. Quickly turning over the pages, he said, "Look here, chum, this is the way to heaven, that verse there, John iii. 16. I'll turn the leaves back, you put your thumb on that verse, and tell him that is the way to heaven."

Quickly Tiny Jim rushed back. He jumped down beside Bert, who lay so still that for a moment he thought he had gone. He touched his shoulder. "I've got it, Bert," he exclaimed. "Here it is, the way to heaven, John iii. 16, 'For God so loved the world, that he gave his only begotten Son, that whosoever believeth in him should not perish, but have everlasting life'."

Poor Bert's eyes were wide open now. He was drinking in every word. What a scene it was—Tiny Jim kneeling on the bottom of the trench, his great hand holding the little Testament, the tears running down his cheeks, reading again and again those life-giving words in the ears of Bert.

A look of peace came over the face of the dying man as he kept gasping out "whosoever". After a bit he lay quiet and still again. Tiny Jim got back on the firing step. All at once he called out, "Look, chaps!" And there was Bert. With one last great effort he raised himself up. He seemed to be gazing at the little piece of blue sky just visible from the trench. His hands were stretched toward it. His face lit up with angelic glory, and with one last gasp, "whosoever", he fell back dead.

Yes, Bert had found the way to heaven. What a change! One moment in a trench on the battlefield, the next with Christ. What about you? Have you, too, found the way? If not, read the verse again. It is the greatest verse in the Bible. Then open your heart to the Lord Jesus Christ and accept Him as your own personal Saviour. Will you do it? Do it—now.

"For God so loved the world, that he gave his only begotten Son, that whosoever believeth in him should not perish, but have everlasting life."

CHAPTER III

THE RICH MAN AND LAZARUS

TURN WITH me, if you will, to the Gospel according to Luke, the sixteenth chapter, verses nineteen to thirty-one.

"There was a certain rich man, which was clothed in purple and fine linen, and fared sumptuously every day: and there was a certain beggar named Lazarus, which was laid at his gate, full of sores, and desiring to be fed with the crumbs which fell from the rich man's table: moreover the dogs came and licked his sores.

"And it came to pass, that the beggar died, and was carried by the angels into Abraham's bosom: the rich man also died, and was buried; and in hell he lift up his eyes, being in torments, and seeth Abraham afar off, and Lazarus in his bosom.

"And he cried and said, Father Abraham, have mercy on me, and send Lazarus, that he may dip the tip of his finger in water, and cool my tongue; for I am tormented in this flame.

"But Abraham said, Son, remember that thou in thy lifetime receivedst thy good things, and likewise Lazarus evil things: but now he is comforted, and thou art tormented. And beside all this, between us and you there is a great gulf fixed: so that they which would pass from hence to you cannot; neither can they pass to us, that would come from thence.

"Then he said, I pray thee therefore, father, that thou wouldest send him to my father's house: for I have five brethren; that he may testify unto them, lest they also come into this place of torment.

"Abraham saith unto him, They have Moses and the prophets; let them hear them.

"And he said, Nay, father Abraham: but if one went unto them from the dead, they will repent.

"And he said unto him, If they hear not Moses and the prophets, neither will they be persuaded, though one rose from the dead."

Not a Parable

This is not a parable. I know that Jehovah's Witnesses say it is, and then invent a fantastic interpretation to suit themselves. They say it symbolises the Jews and the Gentiles. You see, they cannot take it as it reads because it contradicts and overthrows everything that they teach about the future life, and so they have to construe it as a parable.

But it is not a parable. It is a record of an historic fact. Jesus knew this rich man and Lazarus. It really happened just as He told it. It was "a certain rich man", one with whom He was acquainted.

In parables names are never given. Search and see. Never does Jesus give the name of an individual in any of His parables. But here He does. He says the beggar's name was Lazarus. He lived. He was a beggar. He is now with Christ. Some day we will see him. Had this been a parable his name would never have been mentioned. This tragedy occurred. It really happened. Do not think of it then as a parable.

Here are two pictures, one this side the grave, the other, the other side; pictures of two men, the first picture in this world, the second in the next. Let us look at them, for they could easily be pictures of you or of me. What happened to them could happen to us.

The First Picture

In this first picture there is a rich man—a man of the world. He was prosperous and contented. He had all that money could buy. He lived in a mansion, had servants to wait on him, and fared sumptuously every day. Depressions never affected him, for he had abundance.

I have no doubt but that he was highly respected in his community. He had many friends. Rich men generally do. His clothing was of the best, purple and fine linen. He must have held an important position. In any case, he lived in luxury and wanted for nothing.

God did not condemn him for being rich, that is, if he got his riches honestly. He must have been thrifty and industrious. Those who are lazy do not make money. He had used his brains. He had saved. He was not a spendthrift. And he did not idle away his time, taking it for granted that the country owed him a living. He had invested his talents to the best of his ability and had prospered. The Jews, you know, always considered it a sign of God's favour when a man made good. No, there is not a word of censure because he was rich.

The trouble was, as with so many, both rich and poor, he had left God out of his life. He did not feel his need of God. He lived for himself and for himself alone. And he had a heart of stone, for he was unmoved by the sight of poverty right at his door. He showed no mercy. All that he got he kept. He had nothing for others, nothing for God's work. Self-satisfied as he was, he did not take God into account. I have known rich men who have been humble, devoted followers of the Lord Jesus Christ, who have used their money for God's glory and have been a blessing to thousands. But this man had no use for God. God was not in his thoughts.

Now there is another part to this first picture. It portrays a beggar by the name of Lazarus. Day after day he crawls to the estate of the rich man and, unable to stand, lies at his door, hoping for some of the crumbs so eagerly devoured by the hungry dogs under the table. But generally the dogs get there first and the beggar is denied.

Lazarus, almost devoid of clothing, is covered with sores—ugly running sores, all too common in the East. No physician is sent by the rich man to take care of him. No comfortable bed is provided upon which he can rest his weary body. No food is given to him. In fact, he seems to be without friends. But no, he is not alone; the dogs are his companions, for they, too, are hungry, and they seem to be able to sympathize with him. At any rate they gather around and lick his sores. Poor Lazarus! What a tragedy!

Was he always thus? I do not know. Something terrible must have happened to bring him to such depths. Surely it could not have been his own fault. He was not a drunkard. As a matter of fact he was a God-fearing man. He may have had a happy home. But he became ill and lost his job. Finally he got into debt and the creditors came. Perhaps, like Job, his wife turned on him. Yet no complaint does he make. No word of bitterness does he utter. Humbly he accepts his lot and leaves himself in the hands of God. How sublime his faith!

Death

And so they live, the rich man and the beggar. But at last, as with all mankind, life ends and death comes. Both die, first the beggar and then the rich man.

One day the servants notice that the dogs are acting strangely. Some of them look as though they have been knawing on human flesh. They look—and, behold, the emaciated body of the beggar, or what is left of it. Someone dumps it in a ditch, out of sight, and Lazarus is no more. Never again will the rich man be plagued with his presence. Never again will the dogs lick his sores. He is gone and gone forever, or so the rich man thinks, if indeed he thinks at all. "And a good riddance, too," he ejaculates, as he makes his way in his purple and fine linen to his heavily laden table, while his servants hurry to wait on him. Poor Lazarus! No longer will he suffer with the cold. Never again will he feel the pangs of hunger. No more will his sores itch and burn. His poor, nude body, racked by pain, foul and unkempt, is at last stiff and lifeless.

But now it is the rich man's turn, for he, too, must die. He sends for the best physicians, for he is deathly sick. Medicines are prescribed. Every remedy known to medical skill is used. Servants tiptoe back and forth. There upon his luxurious bed he lies, breathing heavily. No effort is spared to save his life. In the grate a fire is burning to keep him warm. Friends and relatives gather round. But it is all of no use. Money cannot save him. The rich man, too, dies.

Lavish are the preparations made for his funeral. It must be one of the best, in keeping with his station in life. No modest Christian funeral for him. The city's most famous undertaker is there. The most expensive mourners are engaged. No such coffin was ever seen before, at least not in his community. It is the best that money can buy. The pall-bearers are his richest and closest associates. They carry it on their shoulders. He is lauded by everyone. And he is buried in his own sepulchre, in the most prominent part of the cemetery— a sepulchre fit for a king. It is a grand spectacle and for days the funeral of the rich man is the talk of the town.

c

"He was buried." Yes, he was buried, while the beggar was not. And that is the end.

The Second Picture

The *END* did I say? Has the story indeed closed? Is there nothing more? What, death the end? NEVER! It would have been had it not been for Jesus. But Jesus saw what transpired immediately after. He could see into the other life. He knew what had happened. He might have ended the story where we would have had to end it, but He didn't. He saw beyond. And Jesus draws back the veil, and now He goes on with the story of the rich man and the beggar. There is another picture. It is a picture of life beyond the grave. Let us look at it.

First of all, Jesus directs our attention to the beggar. He sees him die. So do we. But He sees what happens the moment he leaves his body. We cannot, so He tells us. Jesus sees the angels of God. They are standing near by, invisible to mortal eyes, invisible, as yet, to the beggar himself. They wait for him to draw his last breath and to vacate his tenement of clay.

At last it is all over, his struggles cease, and in a moment he is slipping from his fleshly imprisonment. A moment later and he is free. He looks around. The scenery has not changed. There is the mansion of the rich man. There are the dogs. And there beside him is the body that was once his. Suddenly he glances up, and there, to his amazement, are the angels, and with a glad smile he turns toward them. Eagerly they encircle him. Comforting words are spoken. They bear him aloft. He is conducted to Abraham's bosom, the Paradise of God. Oh, what a scene! What a glorious experience!

My friend, let me pause a moment. Why do you fear death? Do you not know Jesus, and is He not your

Saviour? Then let me say that you have no need to fear.
You will not be alone. Even now the angels are waiting
for you. The moment you close your eyes on this life
they will be there to welcome you. You cannot see them,
but you will see them then. They will show you the way.
You wouldn't know it yourself, but they will guide
you. They will bear you home. Isn't that a comforting
thought? But best of all, it is true. The Word says so,
not only here, but in many places. The angels will be
the first to introduce you to heaven; they will escort
you home.

But what of the rich man? We left him in a rich man's
sepulchre. Now we see him again, as Jesus continues the
story. And where is he? In Hades, the prison house of
hell-bound souls. What is his condition? He is in "torments". And as he suffers, he looks up and sees the
beggar, Lazarus, afar off, in Abraham's bosom. What a
contrast! Yes, and what a calamity!

He is quite conscious, you see. There is no indication
of soul-sleep, nor has he been annihilated. He is there,
and he is conscious of all that is going on around him. He
sees, he hears, he speaks, he feels, he suffers. The unconscious do not see or hear, neither do they speak, feel and
suffer. He is not unconscious.

Prayer in Hades

Now at last the rich man prays. I say at last, for I
doubt if he had ever prayed before. As a matter of fact,
he never before felt the need of prayer. He had all he
required and did not have to ask for anything. At least,
he thought he had, but he was not conscious of his greatest
need, his need of God.

And so now he prays. Why not? There is nothing
wrong with praying, is there? We all need prayer. Prayer

is all right. It is a good thing to pray. But the rich man's praying got him nowhere. What was the matter? Two things.

First, he prayed to the wrong person. He prayed to a saint. "Father Abraham," he cried. Now Abraham was one of the greatest of all the saints. And if Saint Abraham couldn't help him, then what saint could? Why people should pray to a lesser saint when the greatest can do nothing for them, I cannot understand. And yet they do. They pray to all the little saints—Saint Nicholas, Saint Christopher, Saint Joseph, Saint Anthony, Saint Terassah, and, of course, the Virgin Mary. But who are they in comparison to Saint Abraham? If one of the greatest of all the saints cannot help, of what use is it to pray to the lesser saints? Surely if any saint could answer prayer Saint Abraham could. But not a thing could he do. So it is of no use praying to a saint. "There is one God and one Mediator of God and men, the man Christ Jesus" (I Tim. ii. 5), declares the Roman Catholic Bible, and he should have prayed to Him. But he prayed to the wrong person. That was his first mistake.

Second, he prayed too late. He should have prayed while he was still in the body. He should have prayed on earth. But he waited until he had departed from this life and now it is too late. Prayer is never answered in hell. Hades is not the place to pray. And millions are making the same mistake today. They will not take time to pray now, but they will pray in the midst of their misery here-after, and then it will be too late. They will cry, but their cry will be in vain. Their wails will go unheeded there. Now is the time to pray. The rich man prayed too late. That was his second mistake.

His First Petition

In his prayer he offered three petitions, and I want you to note, if you will, how they were dealt with. Here, then, is the first:

"Father Abraham, have mercy on me, and send Lazarus, that he may dip the tip of his finger in water, and cool my tongue; for I am tormented in this flame."

It was a prayer for himself. It was a cry for mercy. "Water! Water!" Not a pailful. Not a cupful. Not even a spoonful. Just a drop. A dip of his finger, not even the hand. And not even the whole finger—just the tip of it. Oh, what desperation! What torture and misery! No water in hell? No, not a drop. Only devouring flames. Unspeakable torment.

I say it was a prayer for mercy. Yes, but he had showed no mercy when he had the opportunity. Not even to Lazarus. His heart was as hard as flint. He knew not the meaning of the word. And now he cries for mercy.

And Lazarus, the beggar—Lazarus who had been beneath his notice on earth—Lazarus whose services he never needed before, Lazarus is now his one and only hope. "Send Lazarus." He was now, he thought, his only friend. Oh, if only Lazarus could help him! And in a wail of agony he offers his first petition.

But now for Abraham's reply. Let me quote it for you in his own words.

"Son, remember that thou in thy lifetime receivedst thy good things, and likewise Lazarus evil things: but now he is comforted, and thou art tormented."

"Son, remember." Remember! Why, that was the very thing that he didn't want to do. Oh, if only he could forget! But that was what tortured him most. Of course he remembered. He remembered his former life, his life of ease and comfort. He recalled all the good things he had once enjoyed. He remembered his days of prosperity, his lovely home, his large bank account, his rich food. He remembered, too, the cool refreshing breeze and the cold days and nights when he enjoyed the warmth of a fire. Yes, and he remembered the beggar, lying at his door, and even the stray dogs. He could see them now as they fought over the crumbs that fell from his table and then turned to lick the nauseating sores that covered the skeleton form of Lazarus. How he wished he could forget! But he had to remember.

You, too, will remember. That is what will make hell really hell. You will remember your sins; they will haunt you, every one. Those deeds done in secret—you will never, never forget them. You will remember the girl you ruined and damned, the little child you abused, your wasted money, and, worse still, your wasted life. You will remember the many times you heard the Gospel and the times you rejected the invitation to accept Christ. You will recall how the preacher pleaded with you and how you left the meeting unsaved. Yes, and you will remember how your mother and how your wife prayed for you. Oh, if only you could forget! But you cannot. You must, and you will, remember.

But that is not the end of the answer. Abraham has more to say yet. He points out that the situation has been reversed, that the rich man, who had enjoyed the good things of life, is now tormented, and that Lazarus, who had known nothing but suffering, is now comforted. Then he continues:

"And beside all this, between us and you there is a great gulf fixed: so that they who would pass from hence to you cannot; neither can they pass to us, who would come from thence."

What does he say? What new revelation is this? A gulf. Something between. Two things about it.

First, it is a *"great"* gulf. I think of the Grand Canyon. To me *it* is a great gulf, yet it might be possible to find a way to cross it. But not this gulf. It is so wide that no one can cross it. It is a *great* gulf. That means eternal separation. That was why the rich man saw Abraham "afar off". He had landed on the wrong side of the gulf and there he had to stay. "In the place where the tree falleth, there it shall be." There can be no crossing over. Destiny is fixed and fixed for all eternity. There is no second chance.

What now have Jehovah's Witnesses to say? The Bible says that the gulf is too great to cross, that no one on the other side can ever get over, that there is no way to bridge the chasm. No second chance! No opportunity of being saved hereafter. The rich man is still there. He has been there for some two thousand years, and there he will remain. He can never, never cross to where Lazarus is. Oh, my friend, beware lest you, too, land on the wrong side, for if you do you will never get over. It is a *GREAT* gulf.

This means that no one can be prayed out once he is in. Buy all the indulgences you like, pay the priest as much money as you can, have prayers offered by the Church and even by the Pope himself, and all will avail you nothing. Abraham says the gulf can never be crossed. You cannot get them out.

Second, it is *"fixed"*: in other words, it can never be removed. The Grand Canyon has been there for thousands of years. This gulf remains forever.. It will never disappear. Millennium upon millennium will come and go, but the gulf will still be there. The saved and the lost will never be united. They will always remain apart. The gulf is *fixed*.

His Second Petition

Now for his second petition. Realizing that his own condition is hopeless, he begins to think of others. And thus he prays:

"I pray thee therefore, father, that thou wouldest send him to my father's house: for I have five brethren; that he may testify unto them, lest they also come into this place of torment."

Now it is a good thing to be concerned about one's relatives, but why wasn't he concerned before? Why didn't he speak to them when he had the opportunity? Why leave it so late? Perhaps his father was still living. I imagine he was. Possibly he was the eldest of the family. Some of his brothers may have been mere children. Be that as it may, he couldn't think of his brothers sharing his doom.

Are we concerned? Do we pray for our relatives now? Or are we, too, going to leave it until it is too late? Perhaps you are not saved yourself and you know you are going to hell. Tell me, do you want your wife to go with you? Do you want your children to suffer as you will suffer? Have you no burden for those you love? My friend, you'd better get anxious now; it will be too late then.

So he prays for his brothers. But now what is Abraham's answer? Marvellous indeed! Listen to it.

"They have Moses and the prophets; let them hear them."

Brief, was it not? Yes, brief indeed, but right to the point. In other words, he said this: "They have the Bible. They have the Word of God. They have the God-breathed writings of Moses and the prophets. Let them hear them."

Oh, the value he places on the Bible! How he honours

the Word! It, he says, is all-sufficient. If they will not listen to the voice of God through His prophets, they will not listen to Lazarus. The Word will be their condemnation.

My friend, you have the Word. If you haven't you can get it. Bibles, Testaments and Gospels are sold and even distributed free of charge in countless millions. What more do you need? It is God's Word you want. It will tell you how to escape hell. It will reveal to you God's salvation. All the information you need is in the Bible. Hence, you are without excuse. No one from the other world can help you. By God's Word you can be enlightened, and by it you can be saved. Yes, and by His Word you will some day be judged. Then hear the Word and listen to what God says: "Faith cometh by hearing, and hearing by the Word of God."

His Third Petition

But not yet is he through, for he is desperate. For himself he knows there is no hope—but oh, those brothers of his—can he not do something for them? He makes one last attempt. He prays once more. Here is his final petition.

"Nay, father Abraham: but if one went unto them from the dead, they will repent."

What desperation! "If one went unto them from the dead." If a miracle could be wrought. If a dead man could be raised. That's it. Let there be a resurrection, something to startle them. "Raise Lazarus and send him to them." Thus he argued and thus he prayed.

Now for Abraham's last words, his final answer:

"If they hear not Moses and the prophets, neither will they be persuaded though one rise from the dead."

A lot of people think that miracles would convince men. But miracles, my friends, only harden. There was another

Lazarus who was raised from the dead, raised after he had been dead four days. Were the rulers convinced? Did that miracle soften their hard hearts? You know it did not. It only made them more determined than ever to get rid of Jesus.

Again Abraham's only answer is the Word of God. It, and it alone, must suffice. If men will not be convinced and saved through it, there is no hope for them. "If they hear not Moses and the prophets", if they reject the Old Testament Scriptures, they must perish. A miracle would not help. The Israelites witnessed miracle after miracle wrought by God through Moses, and still they rebelled, still they murmured and complained. Still they perished in the wilderness. No, says Abraham, not a miracle, but the Word of God. Once they have God's revelation they are responsible.

Not another word is spoken. The rich man is silenced. He has offered his last prayer and now, in horror, he must await the coming of his five brothers, one after the other, unless they repent. The curtain falls and all is over. Ah, but is it? Where is he now? What does he think today?

My friend, you have a choice to make. You can choose to spend eternity with Lazarus or you can go on as you are and finally go to that place of "torments" to which the rich man went. It is for you to decide. But a decision you must make and that soon, or it will be forever too late.

Will you, then, hear the Word of God and open your heart to Jesus Christ, or will you perish in your sin? "Behold, now is the accepted time; behold, now is the day of salvation." You will be "carried by the angels" to your home on high, or you will be "buried, and in hell lift up" your "eyes, being in torments". Which is it to be? It is for you to say.

CHAPTER IV

THE MORNING WATCH

THERE are four words to which I want to call your attention. You will find them in First Timothy, the fourth chapter, and the sixteenth verse: "Take heed unto thyself." These are the words of the Apostle Paul to Timothy and they are of paramount importance: "Take heed unto thyself."

Well did one of the writers of the Old Testament say: "They made me the keeper of the vineyards; but mine own vineyard have I not kept (Song of Sol. i. 6). Many a preacher who cares for the vineyard of others neglects his own. "Take heed unto thyself."

Water can only rise to its own level and no higher. What the preacher is, his congregation will be. Show me a spiritual pastor, and I will show you a spiritual congregation. Show me a worldly pastor, and I will show you a worldly congregation. Show me a carnal pastor, and I will show you a carnal congregation. Show me a soul-winning pastor, and I will show you a soul-winning congregation. Show me a missionary pastor, and I will show you a missionary congregation. "Like priest, like people," said one of old. How true! The people will be what the pastor is.

Suppose you send a carnal missionary to the foreign field and then go out in five years' time and examine his converts. What will you find? You will discover that they, too, are carnal. Suppose you send a spiritual missionary to the field and in five years' time go out and examine his converts. Again, what will you find? You will discover that they, too, are spiritual. "Like pastor, like people." The converts will be what the pastor is. How great, then, is the responsibility of the leader.

"That which is born of the flesh is flesh." That which is born of vegetable is vegetable. That which is born of fruit is fruit. That which is born of fish is fish. That which is born of bird is bird. That which is born of animal is animal. That which is born of man is man. In other words, you cannot cross the species. You can get new varieties, but you cannot get new species. That is why the Bible says: "That which is born of the flesh is flesh, and that which is born of the Spirit is spirit" (John iii. 6).

There again you have the same truth—like pastor, like people. The flesh always remains flesh. Vegetables never become fish. Birds are never changed to animals. "That which is born of the flesh is flesh." Flesh it is, and flesh it always will be. You cannot possibly change it. If you are spiritual, your people will be spiritual. If you are carnal, your people will be carnal. If you are worldly, your people, too, will be worldly. Water, I say, can only rise to its own level, and no higher.

The Level of Your Experience

Herein lies a great lesson, a lesson that but few have learned. You cannot lift others to the level of your preaching, nor can you lift them to the level of your teaching. You can only lift them to the level of your own spiritual experience. They will be what you are. Hence the importance of obtaining and maintaining a deeply spiritual experience of your own. Many a pastor preaches a great sermon and then wonders why the members of his congregation do not rise to the level of his preaching. It is absolutely impossible. They will be what he is. He can lift them to the level of his experience, but he cannot lift them to the level of his preaching.

If you would produce spiritual results, you yourself must be spiritual. You may preach and teach the deepest truths, but you will discover that the lives of those to whom you speak are not being transformed by your preaching, simply because your life does not back up what you say. It is what you are that counts.

God's order is unchangeable. Your pet dog can never become your child. Dog it is, and dog it will always remain, regardless of your teaching and instruction. Fruit always produces fruit and nothing else. "That which is born of the flesh is flesh."

In other words, that which is born of carnality is carnality. That which is born of worldliness is worldliness. That which is born of spirituality is spiritual. Spirituality in you produces spirituality in others. No wonder, then, Paul said to Timothy, "Take heed unto thyself."

That means that the most important part of the sermon is the man who preaches it. The best preparation for the pulpit is an experience with God. The mere theologian will be a failure as a preacher. Everything that interferes with a man's Christian experience interferes with the effectiveness of his sermon. Character is the most important factor of all. Life, not logic, is the essential thing. Experience, and no doctrine, is better than doctrine and no experience. Not only should men prepare their sermons, they should prepare themselves. What a man is conditions the power of what he says.

A sermon illustrated by a godly life is almost irresistible. The preacher's authority is from the unseen Christ, his power from the Holy Ghost. He should so live as to be regarded as a man familiar with the unseen world. His life should be pure and strong as a result of companionship with Christ, for then he will speak with peculiar power.

It is not what he says but what he has experienced that counts. He should practice the presence of God and live a spiritual life.

How Can Spirituality be Maintained?

Well now, how can spirituality be obtained and maintained? If it is of such paramount importance, we must know something of its secret. Let me say that it cannot be obtained at an altar. There is no experience that you can get at an altar that will last you for a lifetime. It is not so easy as that. You will have to pay the price, and I know of but one way to obtain it—at least that has been my experience. Moreover, as I have read the lives of others, those whom God has mightily used, I have come to the same conclusion. They, too, knew no other way.

In the very early years of my Christian life I commenced observing what I have called the "Morning Watch". Every morning, day in and day out, I get alone with God. I would not dream of going to my office before first of all spending time alone with Him. Nor would I attempt to carry on my church work without first meeting God, morning by morning. Directly after breakfast I retire to my study, close the door, and there spend the first hour alone with God. For over forty years now I have observed the Morning Watch. If God has used me in any way down through the years it is because I have met Him morning by morning. I solve my problems before I come to them. Without the Morning Watch my work would be ineffective. I would be weak and helpless. It is only when I wait upon Him that I become strong spiritually.

Years ago I used to think that if I could ever stand before a large congregation and preach the Gospel I would experience the greatest thrill that could ever come to a human heart. Well, for over twenty years now I have had that experience. I do not have to leave my own church to preach to large congregations. For the last twenty years, apart from the hot summer months, I have faced audiences of approximately two thousand both morning and evening. I can stand in my own pulpit Sunday after Sunday and minister to four thousand people. I have travelled all over the world and have faced audiences up to ten and fifteen thousand people in my evangelistic efforts. I say, I have had that experience and I have had it for years.

That thrill, however, has worn off. It wore off long ago. Today it does not mean anything to me to preach to large crowds. It is more or less commonplace. I want to tell you, however, of a thrill that has never worn off. It is the thrill of meeting God morning by morning. Every day I look forward to it. Eagerly I enter my study, morning by morning, to wait upon God. The thrill of the Morning Watch is still as great as ever. It means more to me than anything else in my ministry.

You Must Make Time

You tell me that you do not have time; you are so busy in the work of the Lord that you cannot spare an hour to wait upon Him. Well, Susanna Wesley was busy. She had nineteen children, you remember. And in those days they did not have schools. She had to teach them herself. She could not go to the stores to buy clothes for them. She had to make them. Moreover, she had to provide their daily food. I do not say that she was very busy, but certainly she was busy. She had her hands full. Yet Susanna Wesley every day from one o'clock until two went into her bedroom, closed the door, and there on her knees spent the time alone with God. No child dare interrupt her during that hour. They all knew what she was doing. No wonder Susanna Wesley gave the world John Wesley and Charles Wesley. She knew what it was to get alone with God.

My friend, if Susanna Wesley, busy as she was, mother of nineteen children, could make time to wait upon God, surely you and I, in this day of gadgets, can do the same. We will never get time; we will have to make time. And unless we make time we will not accomplish very much for God.

That is the way we become acquainted with our friends; we take time to meet them, and thus we get to know them. When a young man wants to get married he makes a date, I suppose, with the young woman of his choice. It is hard, of course, for him to spare the time. He realizes that it will mean sacrifice on his part. But, nevertheless, he makes up his mind that it must be done. Somehow or other he must spend an hour or two in her company if he is going to become acquainted with her. He sets aside a certain evening and arranges to call on her. Everything else has to be laid aside, and in spite of the tremendous sacrifice he is making he bravely prepares for the inter- view. She ushers him into her living-room and he sits on one side and she sits on the other side. They never say a word. They just sit there and look at each other. After an hour and a half has passed he says to her, "Well, I guess it's time for me to go now. It's getting late—it's almost ten o'clock." She gives him his hat and his coat and he takes his departure.

Is that the way it is? Not when I was young. She says something to him. He says something to her. They talk to one another. They enjoy each other's company. They look forward with great eagerness to the next meeting, and thus they become acquainted.

So it is with the Lord Jesus Christ. It is so important that you must *make* time if you are going to become acquainted with Him. Thousands there are who have met the Lord Jesus Christ who do not know Him. You have to live with people in order to know them. I met Haile Selassie, the Emperor of Ethiopia. I shook hands with him and photographed him when I was in Africa. I met the Crown Prince, and also the little prince. He came running toward me, begging me to take his picture, as I had taken the picture of his royal father. But I do not know Haile Selassie. I have never lived with him. I have only met him. You met the Lord Jesus Christ when you were converted, but unless you have taken time to become acquainted with Him you do not know Him.

Sometimes you wonder why you cannot rush into God's presence in an hour of need and get His ear. You would never dream of going to a stranger in time of trouble. If you do not know God, and he seems afar off, how can you turn to Him? You have never become acquainted with Him. However, if you have learned to know Him, if you are intimate with Him, then, in your hour of tragedy, you can turn to Him at a moment's notice and He will answer. It will be the most natural thing in the world for you to confide in Him. But you must first know Him. And to know Him takes time. You will have to make time if you are going to become acquainted with Him.

Now how do I observe the Morning Watch? Well, first of all I study the Word, and then I pray.

The Word of God

First, then, I turn to the Word of God. Do you do that? Has there ever been a day in your life since you were converted when you have neglected the Book of books? Have you opened it every day of your life and pored over its sacred pages? Or have there been days

D

when you have failed to read it? I can only remember one day in the last forty years when I have not read it, and on that day I was flying across the ocean and I was very, very ill. I would never dream of going through a day without seeking guidance from God's Word. It is my meat and my drink. Here is my authority: "As new-born babes, desire the sincere milk of the word, that ye may grow thereby" (1 Pet. ii. 2).

One day, just after I had accepted Christ as my Saviour, I was standing at the back of Cooke's Presbyterian Church, Toronto. A personal worker stepped up to me and asked me to loan him my Bible. I did so. He turned to the fly-leaf and he wrote these words: "This Book will keep you from sin, or sin will keep you from this Book." Then he handed it back to me. I think I have written that statement in every Bible I have owned from that day to this, for I found it to be true. Later, I discovered that the one who had originally penned it was the immortal John Bunyan, and after that I signed his name to the statement. The fact of the matter is, sin and the Book cannot co-exist. You will either give up one or the other. If you read the Word of God, you will turn away from sin. If you indulge in sin, you will have no appetite for the Book. "This Book will keep you from sin, or sin will keep you from this Book."

My Bible

May I suggest that you get a Bible with large type, because the day will come when your eyes will grow dim, and then, if you have carefully marked your Bible, you will be glad that the print is large enough for you to still read it. You will not want to cast it aside. Of course, you should always read with a pencil in hand. My Bibles have been marked from Genesis to Revelation. I mark every verse that speaks to my heart. You, too, should mark your Bible.

All down the years of my ministry I have used a Scofield Reference Bible. I have found it more valuable by far than any other. I do not agree with all the notes, but I do agree with most of them, and they have been a wonderful help to me in my Bible study. If I had no other books, I could take a Scofield Reference Bible and travel the world over, and I would have all the sermons I could possibly preach. The Scofield Reference Bible is the King James Version. That version has never been displaced by another, and I doubt very much if it ever will be. It speaks to the heart. Other versions are good to use as references, but if I were you I would stick to the King James Version for my own devotional reading.

You Find it Dry

You tell me that the Bible is dry and uninteresting, and that that is why you do not read it. May I say that the reason you find it dry and uninteresting is because you do not know the Author. As I have already stated, you have met the Author, but you have not become acquainted with Him. Once you really know Him you will enjoy everything that has come from Him.

There was one time a young woman who tried to read a book of poems. She found them so dry and uninteresting, however, that she threw them aside. Later on she met the young man who had written them and fell in love with him. Then once again she picked up the book of poems, and this time, to her utter amazement and astonishment, she found them the most interesting poems she had ever read in her life. What made the difference? They were still the same dry poems they had been before. The difference was in her, not in the poems. She had now met the author, and as she read them she thought of him.

So will it be with you. If you know the Author, the Lord Jesus Christ, you will revel in His Word. It will mean more to you than any other book. The more you read it, the more you will want to read it. There are very few books that I can read more than once. There are a few that I have read twice. There are one or two that I have read three times. Worldly books lose their interest simply because they are written by human beings and are easily understood.

The Word of God is entirely different. It is supernatural. It has come from God. I can never sound its depths. There is always something new in it, something I have not seen before. The more I read it, the more I enjoy it. When I read the Old Testament I read about men whom I am going to see one of these days, and so I want to learn all I can about them. Therefore I find the Old Testament fascinating as well as the New.

How Should You Read It?

Moreover, I read it daily, just as the children of Israel gathered the manna daily. You remember, they could not gather sufficient on one day to do for even two days. They had to go out morning by morning and gather it. That is the only way you can nurture your spiritual life. You will have to study the Word daily. God says "day and night" (Joshua i. 8).

Perhaps you do not read the Word of God because you cannot understand it. You come across passages that are beyond your comprehension. My friend, you should read the Bible as you eat fish. Now how do I eat fish? When I come to a bone, do I take up my plate of fish and throw it away just because I have found a bone? Of course not.

I pick out the bone, lay it on the side of my plate, and go on eating fish. Then, when I come to another bone, I lay it, too, aside and continue eating fish. I am not going to throw my fish away just because I find a bone. Are you going to cast God's Word aside because you come across a passage that you cannot understand? Of course not. Just leave it and go on reading the Word. Lay it aside for the time and continue your study. Keep eating fish. Keep reading the Word.

I read the Word of God as I read a letter. When I get a letter I do not turn to the first page and read a paragraph and then put it away in a pigeon-hole and a week later take it down and read a statement from the third page and then put it back in the pigeon-hole, only to take it out a few days later and look at the signature to see who wrote it. Most certainly not. When I read a letter I start at the beginning, and I read through to the end. Thus I know the contents of the letter. There is no other way to read the Word of God. I appreciate the various booklets that men have compiled, such as the *Daily Light* and others, and I use them. But I would not dream of allowing the *Daily Light* or any other book that man has compiled to take the place of the Bible. If you do that, you will never know the contents of the Book. You must read the Book itself.

I start with the first word of Genesis and I read two or three chapters a day until I have read through to the last word of Revelation. Then the next day I go back to the first word of Genesis and again I read through to the last word of Revelation. How often I have read it I do not know. I have never kept count. But I do know that I have gone through it again and again, reading the entire book from beginning to end. Thus I know something of the contents of the Book. If you really want to know it, you will have to read it like that. You will have to go through it from start to finish. Then you will become familiar with it. Read it, I say, as you would read a letter.

Prayer

When you read God's Word God talks to you. When you pray you talk to Him. Hence, after I have spent some time with the Book I turn to prayer, and thus I observe the Morning Watch. Now this is my authority for prayer in connection with the Morning Watch: "My voice shalt thou hear in the morning, O Lord; in the morning will I direct my prayer unto thee, and will look up" (Ps. v. 3).

Now there are three hindrances to the prayer life, three enemies with which we have to cope. Of course, if you merely fall down at your bedside in the morning and mumble off a few words of prayer, and then get up and hurry to your work, you will not know what I am talking about. Or if you come home at night, mumble off a few words of prayer and then fall into bed, again you will not know what I mean. I am talking about prayer, real prayer, intercessory prayer, prayer that achieves its objective. I say there are three hindrances.

(1) *Interruptions*

Have you ever had the telephone ring when you have been at prayer? Or has the baby cried? Have friends called upon you? Have you been interrupted in one way or another? Satan knows exactly when to send the interruptions. If he can interrupt you when you are at prayer he will have wrecked the efficiency of your prayer ministry.

Now how did I get rid of interruptions? I discovered that I had to have a *time* for prayer and a *place* for prayer. As I have already stated, when I am at home I make my study the place for prayer, and I make the first hour of the morning directly after breakfast the time for prayer. Everyone knows when I am at prayer—therefore interruptions are avoided. You, too, will have to have a place for prayer and a time for prayer. When I am crossing the ocean I find the most secluded part of the deck I can find, and that becomes my place for prayer. When I am at a summer conference I go out into the woods, and there, under the trees, I find a place for prayer. I go back to the same place morning by morning.

May I say that your place for prayer will become so sacred that you will think of it as holy ground. I have stained the walls of my study with the breath of my prayers. I always go back to the same place when I pray, and there God meets me. Have you a time for prayer? Have you a place for prayer? You may not choose the morning. Perhaps some other hour of the day will be more convenient for you. As for me, I have chosen the morning, and I find that if I observe the Morning Watch by having a place and time for prayer I can avoid interruptions.

(2) *Drowsiness*

Have you ever become drowsy when you have been at prayer? You know what I mean. You kneel down and place your head on your arms, close your eyes and attempt to pray. Before very long you become drowsy, and at times you fall asleep. Thus drowsiness hinders your prayer life. Your body is tired and weary. You have become exhausted and you just cannot keep awake.

How did I overcome drowsiness? Let me tell you. I never kneel when I pray. I never stand or sit. I mean, of course, when I am alone, when I am observing the Morning Watch. What do I do, then? I always walk when I pray. I clear the furniture from the centre of the room and then I pace back and forth as I talk to God. I have walked hundreds of miles down through the years as I have prayed. I started doing it at the very beginning of my Christian life and I received so much blessing from it that I have continued it ever since.

Some ministers have to play golf for exercise. I have never had time for such exercise. There has been too much to do. I could not possibly spare the time to get my exercise that way. I find that the very best exercise that one can take is that of walking. Hence, as I walk and pray, I get all the exercise that I need.

Thus I never become drowsy. If I were to fall asleep for a single moment I would crash to the floor and would be wide awake instantly. But that has never happened. As I walk back and forth I am always wide awake. I am on the alert. I am able to pray intelligently, and I never fall asleep. You, too, can overcome drowsiness if you will walk.

(3) *Wandering Thoughts*

You know what I mean. Just when you are concentrating on prayer you find yourself thinking, planning, arranging about the future. Thus Satan fills your mind with wandering thoughts, and instead of praying you are thinking. Well now, how are you going to get rid of wandering thoughts?

I always pray out loud. As I walk back and forth, I put my petitions into words and by praying out loud I avoid wandering thoughts. You see, I have to concentrate upon what I am saying to God just as I concentrate when I am preaching. I have no wandering thoughts when I am in the pulpit. I have to be on the alert. If you will pray out loud, you, too, will find that there will be no wandering thoughts. You, too, will be able to concentrate, and as you put your petitions into words you will be able to pray intelligently by praying out loud.

When you kneel to pray and pray quietly to yourself and to God the time seems long. Perhaps when you open your eyes you will discover that you have only been praying for five or ten minutes. That has been my experience. But when you walk and pray out loud you will discover that the time will go by so fast that you will be amazed. You will open your eyes and look at the clock, and you will discover that you have been praying for half an hour, three quarters of an hour, or perhaps an entire hour. How long do I pray? I pray until I have prayed through. I pray until I have dealt with all my problems, until I have heard from God. Thus prayer becomes an unspeakable delight.

If your friends were to come to visit you, you would never dream of suggesting that they kneel down at a chair and close their eyes. You would want them to stand up before you or sit opposite you, open their eyes, look at you, and talk out loud. You would want to be alert. You would not insult them by failing to give them your complete attention. You would want to be at your very best. Why not do the same when you meet God? Why not be at your best when you are talking to Him? I close my eyes as I walk across the room, just because God becomes more real to me. I may open them for a moment to see where to turn, but immediately I close them again. Thus, as I walk back and forth and pray out loud my problems are solved, and I can go to my day's work directly from the presence of God Himself.

All over the country, and in other countries as well, I have addressed groups of ministers and theological students and I have passed on these suggestions to them. Many a letter have I received stating that their devotional life had been completely revolutionized as a result. They have accepted my suggestions and they have put them into practice, and as a result the Morning Watch has become a reality to them.

Keeping on Top of Your Circumstances

Do you know why so many ministers and professional men have to go to a sanatorium? Let me tell you. It is because they allow their circumstances to get on top of them. Either you will keep on top of your circumstances or your circumstances will get on top of you. If your circumstances get on top of you, then you will go to a sanatorium with a nervous breakdown. If you can keep on top of your circumstances, you can go on indefinitely serving the Lord. The only way I have discovered to keep on top of my circumstances is by observing the Morning Watch. If I do not take time to quietly wait on God, sooner or later my circumstances will get on top of me and I will have a nervous breakdown. However, that has never happened, for during all the years of my ministry I have met God morning by morning. He has solved my problems and has enabled me to keep on top of my circumstances. Thus I have never had a nervous breakdown.

As a matter of fact I have not yet taken a real vacation. I may some day, but up until now I have been preaching week after week, year out and year in, during all the years that have passed and gone. I never expect to retire, nor do I ever think of an eight-hour day. I enjoy my work. I revel in it. It is not work to me, it is play. What you like, you enjoy. There are those who work at football harder than they would work in the factory, and yet they call it play or sport. That is the way it is with me. My work is my recreation. How some can take long vacations and lie around doing nothing I cannot for the life of me understand. No matter where I am, I want to be busy serving the Lord.

Some little time ago I had a serious surgical operation,

but during the five weeks that I was convalescing I had
my dictaphone at my bedside, and altogether I worked
on five different books. One of my mottoes is: "So much
to do, and so little time." Life at best is brief, and there
is so much to be accomplished. How can we be idle? Let
us burn out for God.

No Other Secret

"Take heed unto thyself." This, then, is the secret. I
know of no other. If you are going to obtain and maintain
a spiritual life that will count for God, you will have to
take time and wait upon God. Hence, I suggest, the Morning Watch. Then you will be the kind of a pastor or
missionary you want to be. Your life will tell for God.
There will be something about you that will influence
those around you, so that they, too, will be lifted to the
level of your experience in the Lord Jesus Christ, and you
will bear the kind of fruit God wants you to bear. There
is nothing else so important. I know of no other secret.
There are some ministers who only read the Bible to get
sermons. That is a fatal mistake. They should read the
Word of God for the sake of their own spiritual welfare.
Otherwise they are neglecting their own soul. Unless the
preacher or the missionary feeds on the Word of God
daily, he himself becomes weak spiritually and his
ministry will be ineffective. He must first feed himself,
then out of the abundance of his own spiritual experience
he will be able to minister to others. "Enoch walked with
God." The men who have been the most used of God
have been those who have seen to it that their private
devotions have not been neglected.

It is all summed up in the burning words of the immortal
Bounds: "The man makes the preacher. God must make
the man. The messenger is, if possible, more than the

message. The preacher is more than the sermon. Preaching is not the performance of an hour. It is the outflow of a life. It takes twenty years to make the man. The true sermon is a thing of life. The sermon grows because the man grows. The sermon is forceful because the man is forceful. The sermon is holy because the man is holy. The sermon is full of the divine unction because the man is full of the divine unction. The sermon cannot rise in its life-giving forces above the man. Dead men give out dead sermons, and dead sermons kill. Everything depends on the spiritual character of the preacher."

You see, the preacher or the missionary can be very lazy if he wants to. All he has to do is to prepare two or three sermons a week and visit a few sick people. Unless he takes his calling seriously and creates his own work he will have but little to do, but he can be very busy if he has a mind to work. I am afraid many a minister and missionary spends his time in social events of one kind and another, and never really gets out among the people and does the work to which God has called him, never really labours in the Gospel.

It is so easy to become professional. The man who is preaching for a living will never succeed, but if he is preaching for what he would gladly do for nothing he has caught the vision. God's Word should be a fire burning in his bones. He should preach because he cannot do otherwise. He should labour to get out the Gospel. He must see to it that he does not lose his first love and that he is always on fire. Let him take his work seriously and God will make him a blessing.

That is why I so strongly recommend the Morning Watch. "Take heed unto thyself."

CHAPTER V

HAS THE GOSPEL FAILED?

WHAT a wonderful world this would be if sin could be eliminated! The rich would never again oppress the poor. Every man would be employed; there would be none idle. The labourer would receive a just and adequate wage. Everyone would have all he needed. There would be abundance, and no one would go hungry. Poverty would be unknown. There would be no children working in factories.

There would not be a drunkard anywhere in the world, for men would bring home their wages and spend their money for food and clothing. The appetite for strong drink would be gone. There would be no drunken drivers and no night parties.

Not a single harlot would be found on the streets. All suggestive pictures, statues and paintings would be gone. Nothing unclean would remain. Never again would adultery be committed. Prostitution and White Slavery would be a thing of the past.

There would be no thieves, no bandits or highwaymen. Banks and homes would be safe. Keys and locks would no longer be needed. None would be kidnapped. There would be no jails or penitentiaries; no poor-houses anywhere. Tax payers would be free from all such responsibilities. No one would gamble. Horse-racing, stock-markets and slot-machines would be out of date.

Never again would we hear a man cursing and swearing. God's name would not be taken in vain. None would be angry. Jealousy would be unknown. Never again would anyone be hanged for murder, for such a crime could not be committed, since love would dominate every action. There would be no hate, no selfishness.

Sickness would be gone and death, as we know it, be no more. Never again would there be a funeral, nor a door with crêpe. Every man's word would be trusted; there would be no liars. The dope fiend would be a relic of the dark centuries. War would be no more, for never again would nations fight. Battlefields, armies and navies would be unknown. Peace would reign supreme.

Must Deal With Sin

Oh, what a vision! Do you want it fulfilled? Are you really anxious to make this world a better place to live in? Then you must go the whole way. You must deal with sin, for sin is at the root of all greed and selfishness, all the woes and troubles of the human race—sin, yours and mine.

To deal with sin you will have to go farther and deeper than mere reformation and social regeneration, for sin is a cancer. Only the blood of Christ can cure it. Ignore that, and you have not touched the heart of the disease. Since you and I are both sinners, we must be regenerated as individuals. So must all others. That was why Jesus said, "Ye must be born again." The heart must be changed, its appetites and desires, for "The heart", says God, "is desperately wicked". When the hearts of all men are changed, then, and not until then, we shall have a better world.

That change, the Bible tells us, can come only in part now, for the great majority of men will not accept Jesus Christ as Saviour and Lord. If they would, the Golden Age would be here. But they will not, and hence we have to wait until Christ returns for a better world, for the establishment of the Kingdom of God on earth.

"The blood salvation," said D. L. Moody, "has a wonderful effect upon men's characters. They rarely remain subjects of charity, but rise at once to comfort and respectability. It is the old story of the pig in the parlour. You have to change its nature before it is fit for such an environment. Only the Gospel can do that.

Education has never done it. Nor has reformation. Environment has failed. Cures have all proven useless. There is nothing, my friend, absolutely nothing that has succeeded except spiritual regeneration, and you know it. Regeneration did it for Jerry McAuley, the noted river thief. It did it for John Newton, the African slave trader. It did it for Mary Magdalene, the harlot; for Mel Trotter, the drunkard; and for tens of thousands of others. It will do it for anyone.

Sin, my friend, is the problem—SIN—sin; and Christ is the remedy. All the woes and ills of mankind can be attributed to one thing—sin. Not until you are able to deal with sin will you be able to make this old world a fit place to live in.

My Lord can make drunkards sober. He can make harlots pure. Yes, and He can make the rich generous and employers just. He can transform the dwellers of slums into respectable citizens. He can lift the heavy burdens of life and make sad hearts glad. My Lord, I say, can do all that, as thousands can testify, and infinitely more. He can save His people from their sins.

This World is Doomed

This world is doomed. It is getting darker and darker. The ship is going down. This is Saturday night. The one and only thing for the Gospel preacher to do is to save as many as he can from the wreck. Paul made no attempt to free the slaves. He did not try to reorganize society.

He had no idea of interfering in politics. It was not his mission to better the conditions of the working man, however desirable. His work was to preach the Gospel, to bring souls to Jesus Christ, to implant in their hearts the one and only source of joy and true happiness. And Paul made tens of thousands happy. Moody and Spurgeon came along with the same Gospel and working men everywhere rejoiced in God's salvation.

It is assumed by most agitators that if only higher wages were paid, better homes provided, more leisure given, and living conditions generally made easier, the result would be happiness. My friends, some of the most unhappy people in the world are the rich, the so-called privileged classes. Some of the happiest people that the world has ever known have been men and women in slavery, in abject poverty, or in prison, simply because the spring of happiness is within; it does not depend on outward circumstances.

I have gone to the homes of the poor and destitute and found sunshine and happiness. I have visited the persecuted Christians of Russia, Turkey, Armenia and other countries, and found them the happiest people in the world. I think of Paul and Silas, their feet fast in the stocks, singing praises to God at midnight. I recall the stories of those incarcerated in dungeons during the days of the Spanish Inquisition, the Christians in the catacombs of Rome, men and women in the days of Nero dying in the arenas, and they are all stories of happiness, joy and peace, an experience that the world knows nothing about.

If this life ended all, then we might concentrate on conditions here. But this life does not end all. Compared to Eternity it is brief and of little importance. It is the life beyond the grave that really matters. This life is but a preparation for the life to come, and even if we do suffer here, what does it amount to after all? We are journeying to a better city, a heavenly, and when we reach Eternity the things that we have endured here will fade into insignificance.

That many are poor we readily admit. But Jesus said: "The poor ye have always with you," and we always will, for hundreds of years before God said, "The poor shall never cease out of the land" (Deut. xv. 11). Nor are low wages the only cause. Waste, mismanagement, laziness, extravagance, and especially drink, are very often responsible. Sinful vices of one kind and another are the causes of much of the poverty and ill health of the present day.

The Days of Greatest Progress

Now let me point out that the days of the Church's greatest progress were the days of revivals and soul-saving campaigns. Paul had no message about so-called co-operatives. He was out to win souls, and the Church forged ahead on every side, in spite of the heathenism that surrounded it. His was a day of heroic evangelism. It was when John Wesley and George Whitfield launched their great campaign of evangelism that the Church became strong and powerful. It was during the mighty revival days of Charles G. Finney, C. H. Spurgeon and D. L. Moody that the Church witnessed her greatest triumphs. Countless thousands were made supremely happy, and yet the emphasis was on soul-winning.

When a man one day asked Jesus to interfere and settle a dispute He answered as follows: "Man, who made me a judge or a divider over you?" Yet present-day leaders would have the Church take part in labour disputes and attempt to solve problems that are outside its sphere altogether. "My kingdom is not of this world," exclaimed the Lord Jesus, "for if my kingdom were of this world then would my servants fight." Hence Christ did not

E

propose that He or His Church should mix in the things of the world. We are to be a peculiar people. "Come out from among them and be ye separate, saith the Lord." Does that sound like world conformity? Certainly not.

Therefore, let us keep to our task. Let us preach the Gospel and win souls. We must not be side-tracked. The by-products of Christianity we recognize, and for every improvement we thank God. But our task is to preach the Gospel, gather out the Ecclesia, and leave the establishment of the Kingdom to the King Himself when He returns.

That there will be a millennium there can be no doubt. A Golden Age is promised. For the knowledge of the Lord will cover the earth as the waters fill the seas. The time is coming when there will be no more war. The Kingdom will be established on earth, and the prayer "Thy Kingdom Come" will never again have to be offered.

That time cannot be until Jesus Christ takes over the reins of government. There can be no Kingdom without a King. And to establish the Kingdom upon earth before the King Himself appears is impossible. Not until the Prince of Peace reigns will the earth be governed in righteousness. Hence the establishment of the Kingdom is not the work of the Church. The Gospel has not failed.

CHAPTER VI

ONLY TWO GROUPS

THERE are just two groups in this world of ours today—those who *have heard* the Gospel and those who *have not;* those who *can* hear and those who *cannot.* And so far as I am concerned I am for those who have not. Untold millions are still untold.

When I think of the Gospel radio programme, the tens of thousands of churches, the millions of tracts, the great evangelistic campaigns and the multitudes of Christian organizations and workers here in the homeland, and then compare it with the almost complete absence of them among the tribes and peoples still untold, my whole soul revolts within me at the shame of it, the unfairness and injustice.

In a certain city a missionary turned on the radio and got a Gospel programme. He turned the dial and got another. Again he turned it and got a third. There were over forty religious broadcasts on the air that day. Think of it—the same Gospel to the same people at the same time! What overlapping! And all supported by God's money, money that might have been used to broadcast the Message in a foreign land. Is it fair? Is it right? What must God think of us?

Where Should We Labour?

If there were two companies of people before me, one that had not eaten for a week and the other having had three meals a day, to which company would I offer food? To those who had eaten, or to those who had not? The answer is obvious. Can I then give my money for work in the homeland, or ought I to give it for the sending of missionaries to those who have never heard? Some day God will demand an accounting. Why should we force the Gospel upon those who have rejected it, when there are still millions who have never even heard it?

There is a popular song today called "It is No Secret" and it says "It is no secret what God can do". But it is. To countless millions it is still a secret. They do not know what God can do. They do not know because they have not been told.

"Faith cometh by hearing, and hearing by the word of God." But "how shall they hear without a preacher"— or a missionary? "And how shall they preach except they be sent?" (Rom. x. 17, xiv. 15). There is no other way. How many have you sent? What have you done? Do you give all your money here at home where there is so much over-lapping, or are you sending out substitutes to the regions beyond? Are you going to labour here where labourers are treading on each other's toes, or are you going to labour out there where you will have no competition? When a church here became vacant two hundred pastors tried to get it. Out there each one could have had a whole tribe.

Well now, what are we going to do about it? There is just one question that we need ask. Have they heard or have they not? Can they hear or can they not? If they have, then let us think twice before giving more of our money. If they have not, and cannot, then we have a challenge to meet, a work to do, and a job to complete.

I say again, there are only two groups—those who *have heard* and those who *have not,* and you must identify yourself with one or the other. WHICH IS IT TO BE? Why should anyone hear the Gospel twice before everyone has heard it once?

Good Enough For Them

But are not their own religions good enough for them?
Why then disturb them? Why send missionaries to the
heathen? Leave them alone. They are far happier as
they are. Their own religions are good enough for them.

Such are the statements we hear on every side. Such
are the objections that are raised to missionary work.
Travellers come home and tell us that the heathen are
perfectly happy and contented as they are, and that the
work of the missionary is unnecessary.

But we do not think that their own liquor is good enough
for them. Oh no, we ship them ours. Nor is their own
tobacco good enough for them. They must have our
cigarettes. Their own education is not good enough either,
so we give them ours. Their medical work also is inade-
quate, and so ours is substituted. Even their agricultural
methods won't do, so the United Nations introduce ours.

Now the Bible says that "the dark places of the earth
are full of the habitations of cruelty" (Ps. lxxii. 20). And
so it is. The trouble is, the tourists do not stay long
enough to find out. Heathenism is characterized by
cruelty. Fear grips their hearts. They are in constant
dread of evil spirits, spirits that must somehow be
appeased.

Africa

I am thinking now of my visit to Africa and the story
I was told. It was at midnight. Suddenly there was a
death wail in the village; a little baby had died. Immediately the witch doctor was called. The villagers were
aroused. Before very long he had pointed out a woman
whom he accused of having caused the death of the little
one. She immediately protested, insisting that she was

innocent, but she had to be tried. They hurried her away to the tree that stood in the centre of the village. She was told to climb it and then hurl herself from the topmost bough. She began to climb. Presently she sat on one of the branches and again protested her innocence. Everyone knew she was telling the truth. She was one of the finest women in the village, highly respected by all, but the witch doctor had pointed her out as the one guilty, hence she had to prove her innocence.

Then she commenced climbing again, until she had reached the very highest limb of the tree. There she sat, again maintaining her innocence. Then, before the horrified gaze of the missionary, she threw herself down to the hard ground and was instantly killed, most of the bones of her body being broken. She was thereby judged guilty. Had she been innocent she would have been unharmed.

That, my friends, has happened in the case of hundreds upon hundreds. WHY? Because of religion. Heathen religions demand it, hence there is no escape. Would you be willing to take her place? Until you are prepared to accept her religion and give up your Christianity let no one ever hear you say, "Their religions are good enough for them." If they are not good enough for you, then they are not good enough for them.

Australia

I am thinking of my visit to the aborigines of Australia. Away back in the heart of that Continent there is an immense desert where it gets very hot, and there the aborigines live, almost naked—oftentimes sleeping on the sand. A mother gives birth to a baby. Someone in the village dies. A victim must be found.

Before long the witch doctor makes his way towards the new-born babe. The mother clutches it frantically to her breast, but without a moment's hesitation the witch doctor tears it from her arms and, amid her shrieks and cries, lays it on its back on the sand, forces open its little mouth, takes handfuls of sand and pours it into the open mouth and down the throat, until its mouth is filled with sand and the little thing strangles to death. WHY? Because their religions demand it. There must be a human sacrifice. Evil spirits have to be appeased.

Would you be willing to change places with that mother? If her religion is good enough for her, then it is good enough for you. But unless you are willing to take her place and have your little new-born baby torn from your arms and put to death, as hers was, you have no right to say that their religions are good enough for them. It is because of religion that these horrible practices are carried on.

Do you not think that the mother suffers, just as you would suffer? Of course she does. She feels for her baby as you would feel for your baby, but the witch doctor knows no mercy; the spirits must be satisfied. Is her religion good enough for her? Then it is good enough for you. Does her religion make her happy? Could you be happy under such circumstances?

The South Sea Islands

I am thinking, too, of my visit to the South Sea Islands. John Geddes was one of the first missionaries to go to the South Sea Islands from Canada. It was years ago now. As he stepped ashore he saw a group of people, and on the ground the body of a man. Under a tree he saw a young woman. She was the widow of the man who had died.

Suddenly the natives approached her. She was unresisting. Full well she knew what would happen. They placed a cord around her neck, and then commenced to strangle her to death. John Geddes rushed towards her in an effort to rescue her, but he was rudely pushed away and told to mind his own business and that if he didn't he, too, would lose his life. And there before his horrified eyes he saw that beautiful young woman slowly strangled to death and her body placed beside that of her husband.

WHY? Because their religion demanded that when a husband died his widow must be strangled to death to accompany him on his journey. And if the eldest son is old enough he is the one who must strangle his mother. Moreover, all the children, if they are too young to support themselves, must likewise be put to death. That is religion, heathen religion.

Would you be willing, my friend, to change places with that widow? Could you look forward to such an experience in the event of your husband's death? If their religions are good enough for them, then they are good enough for you; and if they are not good enough for you, then do not say that they are good enough for them.

India

Never will I forget my visit to India. Many a time, as I walked by the side of the river, did my mind go back to that day when the body of the husband was placed on a pile of wood, and then the widow, still alive and well, placed beside him, and the two bodies, one dead and the other alive, bound together, and then the whole set on fire. There, amid the shrieks and screams of the dying widow as she slowly burned to death, the natives gathered around, believing that the evil spirits were being pacified, and that now the husband would have his wife in the other life.

Do you mean to say that you would be willing to change

places with that widow? Thousands upon thousands of widows died in the flames when their husbands died, just because of religion. Are their religions good enough for them? Then they must also be good enough for you. If you, my friend, would not be willing to exchange places with that widow, giving up your Christianity and taking her heathen religion, then do not say that their religions are good enough for them and that they are better off as they are. Could a widow be happy enduring such torture? Of course not. "The dark places of the earth are full of the habitations of cruelty."

Twin Babies

Have you ever known of twin babies to be spared in Africa? Never in heathenism. They are always put to death. Would you be willing to have your babies, if they happened to be twins, murdered before your eyes? That is what happens in Africa. The witch doctor immediately sees to it that they are destroyed. No twin babies are allowed to live. Why? you ask. Just because their religions demand it.

Would you be willing to change places with them? Are their religions good enough for them? Then they must also be good enough for you. Such is heathenism, and such are the sorrows of the heathen.

Mohammedanism

Will I ever forget the story of that Mohammedan who stood before the people in the centre of the town and hacked his skull with a great, long knife until the blood flowed freely, and then took newspapers and stuck them into those open gashes, after which he deliberately struck a match and set the whole on fire? There he stood, the fire sizzling the blood, burning the paper and the hair; the man enduring the most excruciating agony.

Why? you ask. Because of his religion. He must afflict his body; he must suffer; he must endure torture in order to gain a place in heaven, and so he tormented himself. Would you be willing to exchange places with him? Would his religion be good enough for you? Could you endure such torment? Would you be willing to suffer as he suffered? Oh, my friend, unless his religion is good enough for you, do not say that it is good enough for him.

Indo-China

Come with me to Indo-China. We are among the tribes-people. A helpless little girl is lying on her back, her head firmly held between the knees of an inhuman monster, who with a coarse saw is deliberately sawing her beautiful front teeth off at the gums. The perspiration stands in beads upon her almost naked body as she endures the dreadful pain. Nerves are exposed. Blood pours from her mouth. Pain, indescribable, is endured, until at last the hideous, barbarous operation is over and she is released, to live her life with nothing but ugly gums. Would you change places with her? What about your own little girl? Would you want her to suffer such torture? Yet countless thousands have borne it and all because of a heathen religion, little innocent victims, unable to escape. That is heathenism. If such a religion is good enough for them, it is good enough for you.

A Little Girl

Or come again to dark, benighted Africa. Once more it is a little girl, this time a baby. The cruel, heartless monster takes his knife and cuts her lovely face from the head to the middle of her body, in great long gashes, sometimes more than a hundred of them. The little one screams in agony. Blood pours from the cuts. Then something is rubbed in to make them fester and produce long, ugly ridges that she will wear as long as life lasts. Oh, what torture! What awful pain and suffering! But there is no escape. It has gone on for centuries; it is going on now. And all in the name of religion. When will it end? How long, O Lord, how long? Would you change places with her? Are you ready to accept such a diabolical religion? Do you think the heathen are better off as they are? Then you have no heart. God have mercy upon you.

The heathen are NOT better off as they are. They are NOT happy, they are miserable. They are most unhappy, they are wretched, they suffer, they are in fear of evil spirits constantly, they are always attempting to appease them. There is no rest in heathenism, no peace, no joy. Only Jesus Christ can impart joy. Therefore let us do everything we possibly can to give them the Gospel before it is forever too late, that they may experience the joy that you and I know in Christ. Let us never again say, "THEY ARE BETTER OFF AS THEY ARE. THEIR RELIGIONS ARE GOOD ENOUGH FOR THEM."

Tragic but Hopeful

This, then, is the other group, those who have not. This is heathenism. They have not heard; they cannot hear. They are without hope. Fear dominates their lives. Suffering is their lot. Always they are under the control of evil spirits.

When Mary Slessor first went to Africa she found herself among cannibals. Human sacrifices were offered. When a chief died heads were cut off, wives buried alive or killed and eaten. Hands were dipped in boiling oil.

Only the Gospel has changed all this. But, thank God,

it has. And oh, what Christians they make! Alexander Mackay tells of the three boys who died for Christ. Their ages were twelve to fifteen. The eldest stepped forward singing a gospel hymn. They cut off his arms, and then threw him into the fire and burned him alive. They did the same with the second. Then came the turn of the youngest, only twelve. "Please don't cut off my arms," he pleaded. "I will not struggle. Just throw me into the fire." What heroes!

In the South Sea Islands there is a tablet. It was erected to the memory of John Geddes, and this is the inscription on it: "When he landed in 1848 there were no Christians here, and when he left in 1872 there were no heathen." Such is the power of the Gospel.

Again I say, there are only two groups, those who have heard and those who have not; those who can hear and those who cannot. Nor are the religions of the heathen good enough for them. Oh, then with which will we work? Where will we go? To what shall we give? I leave it with you to decide, for "how shall they hear without a preacher? And how shall they preach except they be sent?"

CHAPTER VII

THE DEITY OF JESUS CHRIST

THE BIBLE most emphatically speaks of Jesus as God. Therefore if you are going to take issue on the deity of Christ you will have to discard the Scriptures. For nearly two thousand years the Church Universal has believed that the Scriptures affirm the deity of Jesus. Only the false cults have ever denied it.

There are only two possible alternatives. Jesus Christ was either a mere man or else He was what He claimed to be—the Son of God. But since He claimed to be the Son of God, then if He was only a mere man He was an impostor and a deceiver.

If He was an impostor and a deceiver, He was a liar, unworthy of our reverence, unsafe as a guide and teacher, and imperfect as an example. Which means that if He was a mere man He was not the noblest and best, the finest and highest specimen of the human race.

Such a man I, for one, would not follow. I do not want an impostor and deceiver for my example. A man who was not what He Himself claimed to be is not going to win my respect.

Jesus Christ was not a mere man; hence He was not an impostor and deceiver. He was none other than what He claimed to be, the unique and only begotten Son of God. And that, I say, the Word of God affirms again and again.

He was not "a" son of God, as you and I are by regeneration; He was "the" Son of God, or, as the Scriptures state it again and again, "the only begotten Son of God" by nature, very God of very God.

Arius was the first heretic to attack the Person of our Lord. He taught that Christ was neither God nor man but a created Being between the two, the first and the noblest of God's creations, but inferior in power and glory to the Father. Fierce and long the battle raged, until the whole Church was rent asunder. Finally, in A.D. 325, the Nicea Council was called by Constantine the Great, Emperor of the Roman world, over which he himself presided. It met at Nice and lasted for over two months. Athanasius took up the fight against Arius and his followers.

The Council, by an overwhelming majority, affirmed its belief in the deity of Christ, stating that He was "of the same substance with the Father", and Arius was excommunicated. The bishops were convinced that the Christ who was their Saviour could not be less than God. From that day to this the Church has held that the Bible teaches the deity of Jesus Christ. Only the false cults still side with the heretic Arius.

In Matthew xxii. 41–5, we read these words: "What think ye of Christ? whose son is he? They say unto him, The son of David. He saith unto them, How then doth David in spirit call him Lord, saying, The Lord saith unto my Lord, Sit thou on my right hand, till I make thine enemies they footstool? If David then call him Lord, how is he his son?" See also Acts ii. 34–6.

Does a father call his son his Lord? Never! But David did. He spoke of the Messiah as his Lord, and predicted that He would sit on God's right hand and that His enemies would become His footstool. Hence He was more than a son—He was his Lord and his God.

Well then, was Jesus Christ born of man or of God? If Joseph was His father, then He was not the Son of God. If He was conceived by a Roman soldier, or any other man, He was not conceived of the Holy Ghost. If He had an earthly father He had a sinful nature, so that He could not become man's Saviour. Only the God-man could redeem men. Jesus Christ was virgin born, therefore He was God the Son.

"According to Scripture," writes Dr. Ironside, "Christ Jesus is God from all eternity, the ever-living uncreated Word (John i. 1), whose glorious title is the Son, the Creator of the world and all things, who upholds all that exists (John i. 3, 10; Col. i. 13–17; Heb. i. 1–3)." By this test all cults stand or fall.

> *"What think ye of Christ? is the test*
> *To try both your state and your scheme:*
> *You cannot be right in the rest,*
> *Unless you think rightly of Him."*

First, Jesus is Called God

The Bible again and again speaks of Jesus as God. He is called God.

(1) Our first passage is Matthew i. 23. "Behold, a virgin shall be with child, and shall bring forth a son, and they shall call his name Emmanuel, which being interpreted is, God with us." Hear it again—"God with us". Jesus was God, His name was Emmanuel, "God with us". So He is called God.

(2) Look next at John i. 3. "The Word was God." There is the eternal, ever-present "was". Jesus always was and always will be God. In verse 14 John says that "The Word became flesh and dwelt among us"—the same Word, note; in the Greek, the Logos. The Christ who appeared in flesh and tabernacled among men, John says, "was God". That should settle it. Weymouth translates the second verse, *"He* was in the beginning", proving "the Word" to be Christ.

Even when speaking of His incarnation John had to state that he had beheld His glory, the glory as of the only begotten of the Father. Yes, he had seen Him in His glory. It was on the Mount of Transfiguration, and he never could forget the outshining of His deity. Peter, too, recalled that marvellous sight on the holy mount. And that same divine glory John saw again when he beheld Him on the Isle of Patmos. Yes, "the Word was God".

(3) But look now at John i. 18. Let me read it from the Centenary Translation: "No one has ever seen God; God, only begotten, who is in the bosom of the Father—he has interpreted him." What a statement! How absolutely convincing in the original! The Word incarnate, Jesus Christ, is now called "God, only begotten", and He is still one with the Father, for it speaks of Him as being "in the bosom of the Father", though incarnate. It is not "the only begotten Son", as in the Authorized; it is "the only begotten God".

Hence He could say, "He that hath seen me hath seen the Father" (John xiv. 9), and "He that seeth me seeth him that sent me" (John xii. 45). To look at Jesus was to look at God, for He was God, God veiled in human flesh, "God, only begotten". In these remarkable statements is asserted in the most direct manner the full deity of the incarnate Word.

(4) Our next passage is found in John xx. 28, where Thomas cries, "My Lord and my God." Here again Jesus is called God. Has ever a man been addressed thus? Of course not. Such an exclamation, if spoken to a mere mortal, would be nothing short of blasphemy. Thomas recognized Him as God and rightly so.

(5) Now let us examine Romans ix. 5. The best translation of the Greek, according to most authorities, is the Berkeley version. "There are the fathers, and from them in human lineage sprang Christ, he who is God over all, blessed forever." Here Jesus Christ is again called God, "God over all". How, then, can man doubt His deity?

(6) We turn next to Titus ii. 13. To get the best translation I read from the Centenary. "We look for the blessed hope and epiphany of the glory of our great God and Saviour Jesus Christ." Not only is He here called God, He is designated "our great God". So once again Jesus Christ is God. Who, then, is man to deny it?

(7) Now let us turn to Hebrews i. 8. "But unto the Son he saith, Thy throne, O God, is for ever and ever." Here God the Father speaks to the Son and He calls Him God. "Thy throne, O God." Could language be plainer? Jesus is God.

(8) In 2 Peter i. 1 we have the expression "Our God and Saviour Jesus Christ". Our Authorized Version does not translate it correctly. But in the Roman Catholic Bible, the Revised Standard Version, James Moffatt, Berkeley, and the Centenary, Jesus is called "our God". Hence Peter, who knew Him well, recognized Him as God. The word "God" as used here does not mean the Father, it means the Son.

(9) We turn now to 1 John v. 20. It says in this verse, "He is the true God", referring, of course, to Jesus Christ. I have again quoted from the Centenary Translation. This is one of the strongest statements in the Bible. John, now an old man, who in his youth was closely associated with Christ in the flesh, calls Him "the true God". What a confession! He was in very deed God the Son, the second Person of the Trinity, very God of very God; in a word—"true God". 2 John 9, "the Son as . . . God" (Phillips).

(10) Look at Revelation i. 8. Who is speaking? Jesus Christ (i. 1). Who is to come? Jesus Christ (i. 7–8). What does He say? "I am Alpha and Omega." He is from eternity to eternity, without beginning and without end. He always was; He always will be. He is, He was, He is to come. He is the Almighty. Could words be plainer?

He is God. It is not the Father who is to come, it is the Son. So it is the Son who claims to be the Almighty. See Revelation xxii. 13, where the same expression is again used by the Son. What a revelation of His deity!

Need I point out that in Isaiah ix. 6–7 Jesus is called "THE MIGHTY GOD"? Could any writer make a stronger statement? Does not Isaiah here call Him God?

Jesus spoke of Himself as God. In John viii. 24, 28, 58 and xiii. 19 He called Himself "I AM", one of the greatest of the Old Testament names for God. "He" is in italics. He just said "I am". He, Jesus, was none other than the great "I AM".

In Mark x. 18 Jesus says, "Why callest thou me good? There is none good but One, that is, God." Was Jesus good? Of course He was. He was of the very essence of goodness. "In Him is no sin" (1 John iii. 5). Of no other could that be said. Then, being good, He was God. What a claim! In other words, "If I am good, I am God."

Look, too, at John x. 30–3. When He said that He and the Father were "One" the Jews took up stones to stone Him. What for? "Blasphemy," they said. "Thou makest thyself God." They knew what He meant; He was claiming to be God. It was for this claim that He was put to death.

In 1 Timothy iii. 16 it is said of Him that He was "God manifest in the flesh". What a clear and emphatic statement. Zech. xiv. 5 says, "The Lord my God shall come," namely, Christ.

In Hebrews i. 2–3, 10–12, He is the Creator and sustainer of all things. He sits on God's throne and He is from everlasting. Who could He be but God? See John i. 3–10.

There are many other such passages. Again and again Jesus is called God, but these are sufficient. If you, my friend, will not be convinced by these, then it would be useless to quote others. You will have to continue in your heresy and perish in your unbelief, for your Arianism can never face the light of the Word. Jesus is called God.

Second, Jesus is Called the Son of God

In numerous passages Jesus is called the Son of God, and in each instance it is a claim to deity. That the Jews so understood it is proved by the fact that they accused Him of blasphemy and declared Him to be worthy of death. As the son of a king partakes of royal blood, so the Son of God partakes of deity. He was the unique and only begotten Son of God, born, not of Joseph, but of the Holy Ghost, and being virgin born He was the Son of God as no one else ever can be. The Jews always thought of the Messiah as God's Son and therefore divine. If He was the son of an earthly father, then He was not the Son of God.

Jesus was God's *only* Son. He Himself said so when referring to Himself in Mark xii. 6, "Having yet therefore one son, his well beloved, he sent him." In John i. 14, 18; 1 John iv. 9 and many other passages He is spoken of as "the only begotten Son". Men may become children of God in time by adoption. He was the Son of God in eternity by nature. He was not A son; He was THE Son.

The angel Gabriel called Him the Son of God. "The Holy Ghost shall come upon thee, and the power of the Highest shall overshadow thee; therefore also that holy thing which shall be born of thee shall be called the Son of God" (Luke i. 35). Was ever such an announcement made to another? Never! It was in the womb of Mary that Christ became a babe and took upon Him human flesh. He was the one and only Son of God ever born of woman.

John the Baptist called Him the Son of God. "This is the Son of God" (John i. 34). Thousands came to him to be baptized in the River Jordan, but of no one else did he ever make such a statement. Of all those who came, Jesus alone was recognized by him as the Son of God.

Nathaniel called Him the Son of God. "Thou art the Son of God" (John i. 49). There is no record that he ever said that of another.

God called Him His Son. "This is my beloved Son" (Matt. iii. 17, xvii. 5 ; Mark ix. 7). Of all the millions who have lived He was the only one to whom the heavens opened and who heard such a pronouncement.

Demons called Him the Son of God. "Jesus, thou Son of God" (Matt. viii. 29). "Thou art Christ the Son of God" (Luke iv. 41). How was it that they recognized Him so quickly? We never hear of them making a mistake and calling anyone else God's Son. He and He alone was so designated. See also Mark v. 7. Weymouth says they "screamed" out at Him (Mark i. 23, 24). Why did He affect them so? No one else ever did.

Satan tempted Him on the basis of His Sonship. "If thou be the Son of God," he cried (Luke iv. 3, 9). Did he ever tempt another thus? Of course not. He knew full well that Jesus was in very deed the unique Son of the Almighty. Satan never spoke of another as God's Son.

Peter called Him the Son of God. "Thou art the Christ, the Son of the living God" (Matt. xvi. 16). Peter was well acquainted with his brother Andrew and the other disciples, and well he knew that they were children of God, but he never singled out any one of them and called him the Son of God. See also John v. 23.

John believed Him to be the Son of God. In numerous passages he called Him the Son of God, both in his Gospel as well as in his epistles, and in 1 John iv. 15 he plainly states that only those who believe Him to be God's Son are really saved. He always sets Him forth as the one and only Son, the "only begotten of the Father". It was to prove the deity of Jesus that John wrote his Gospel. "Jesus is the Christ, the Son of God," he states (John xx. 28).

Jesus Himself claimed to be the Son of God. One reference will suffice, since it is unanswerable. In Mark xiv. 61-4 we are presented with a most amazing scene. The high priest challenges Him with the question, "Art thou the Christ, the Son of the Blessed?" Jesus could not remain silent. His answer was immediate and final. There was no mistaking His meaning. He simply said, "I am." That settled it. Jesus Himself claims to be God's Son. No wonder the priest "rent his clothes" and called His answer "blasphemy". No wonder they judged Him worthy of death. They all claimed to be children of God, every one of them, but full well they knew what He meant when he said that He was the Son of God. No one else would ever have answered as Jesus answered. See also Matthew xxvi. 62-6.

Even the thieves knew that He claimed to be the Son of God, for they said, "If thou be the Son of God" (Matt. xxvii. 40). So, too, the chief priests were familiar with His claim, for they quoted Him as saying, "I am the Son of God" (Matt. xxvii. 43). And Jesus Himself said this, "I said, I am the Son of God" (John x. 36). Moreover, the chief priest stated that "He ought to die, because he made himself the Son of God" (John xix. 7). And in John v. 25, xi. 4, and Rev. ii. 18 he definitely calls Himself the Son of God.

"Dost thou believe on the Son of God?" inquired Jesus of the man born blind. "Who is he, Lord?" asked the man. And the reply of Jesus was: "It is he that talketh with thee" (John ix. 35-8).

Jesus never recognized an earthly father. Not once did He call Joseph His father. Why not? He should have if he were. His claim throughout His life was that God was

His Father, and that therefore He was God's Son. "Thy father and I," said Mary. "My Father's business," replied Jesus (Luke ii. 48, 49). Mary spoke of Joseph. Jesus ignored Joseph and spoke of God as His Father. In Mark vi. 13 He is spoken of as "the Son of Mary". Why not as "the son of Joseph"? Because He was not. He was the Son of God.

Then in Matthew xxviii. 19 the Son is the second person in the Trinity. It is the "name", singular, not "names". One God in three persons.

In this connection look at John v. 18. It is simply tremendous in its implication. "Therefore the Jews sought the more to kill him, because he . . . said . . . that God was his Father, making himself equal with God." Would they have tried to kill you had you called God your Father? Of course not. Why? Because with you it would not have been a claim to deity, to equality with God. You would simply be saying that you were God's child by regeneration, as millions of others are. But when He said it, He meant, as they well knew, that He had no earthly father, that He had come from heaven, that He was indeed the promised Messiah, the unique and only begotten Son of God, and that therefore He was divine.

Look at it—equality with God. Yes, that and nothing less. "All men should honour the Son, *even as* they honour the Father," He said. "He that honoureth not the Son honoureth not the Father which hath sent him" (John v. 23). Thus Jesus places Himself on the same level as His Father by using the words "even as". He claimed for Himself the honour due to God alone. Then if He was equal to God, He was God, for He was of the same substance as God. But they did not believe in His deity, and so they accused Him of blasphemy and condemned Him to death. Think of anyone else making such a claim. Impossible! Absurd! Only Christ could have uttered such a statement, for He was and is God—God the Son.

Nowhere in the Bible is this equality with God stated more plainly or definitely than by Paul in Philippians ii. 5–11. This is the great classic passage regarding the deity of Christ. In exhorting the Philippians to emulate the unselfishness of their Lord, Paul points out that although He was in His very nature God, yet He humbled Himself and lived as a man. But He was not by nature man; by nature He was God, and He could have lived as God. Paul says He was "in the form of God", not of man, nor of angels, but of God, thus announcing His equality with God. Hence He was all that God is. While on earth He voluntarily lived a life that was not His by nature, for He was still God. There is no suggestion that He ever laid aside His deity.

Now let me quote it from the Centenary Translation: "Christ Jesus, who, though from the beginning he had the nature of God [not angels or men, note, but God], did not reckon equality with God [which was His] something to be forcibly retained, but emptied himself of his glory [not His deity]." It was His glory that He laid aside. Finally He returns to His former state, and everyone in Hades, on Earth and in Heaven bows to Him, bows because He *is* God. Then in Colossians i. 15–19 again He is in the form of God, not man or angels. He is the Creator of everything and He holds the universe together, for He is God.

What does He mean, then, when He says, "The Father is greater than I?" (John xiv. 28). Greater in what? He does not say. Certainly not in nature. Obviously in condition. Look at the entire verse. His disciples were sorrowful because He was leaving them. He tells them that if they only knew how much better heaven is than earth, His Father's condition above than His beneath, they would rejoice. So He is simply speaking about His condition at the time on earth and His Father's in heaven, and of course His Father's condition was greater (more to be desired) than His. But soon He returned to His Father and then His condition was equal to His Father's, for again, as He had prayed, He shared the glory that had been His with the Father "before the world was" (John xvii. 5).

A Number of Things to Explain

If Jesus Christ was not God, if He was merely a man, then you have a number of things to explain that cannot be explained. Grant Him deity and the explanation is simple; deny His deity, and you are at a complete loss.

(1) *His pre-existence*

Proverbs viii. 22–31 can refer to nothing less than the eternal Son of God. This is Christ and He is declared to be from everlasting—from the beginning. Only a person can rejoice and experience delight. Wisdom is here personified. Hence He did not begin to live when He was born. He always was.

Micah v. 2 says of Christ: "Whose goings forth have been from of old, from everlasting." That should settle it. Jesus, who had lived from all eternity, took upon Him the body of a babe, lived among men for a few years, and then returned to where He had been from all eternity.

"In the beginning was the Word, and the Word was with God, and the Word was God. The same was in the beginning with God. All things were made by him; and without him was not any thing made that was made. And the Word was made flesh, and dwelt among us" (John i. 1–3, 14). And that statement, my friend, is all-inclusive, nor can it be misunderstood. The Word was Christ; He was in the beginning, He was God, He created all things,

He became flesh and dwelt among us—Jesus. See John i. 1, 2; ii. 13.

In John i. 15 John says, "He was before me." He existed before John was born. Now John was born before Jesus and therefore was the elder of the two and yet John declares that Jesus lived before he did. He refers, of course, to His pre-existence. That statement he repeats in verse 30: "He was before me."

"Down from heaven"—these words are used seven times in John vi. Then in verse 62 Jesus announced that He would "ascend up where he was before". So the One who said "I came down from heaven" evidently knew that He did not begin life on earth. His home had been in heaven. He had "come down", and He looked forward to returning, all of which is positive proof of His pre-existence.

In John viii. 58 He says, "Before Abraham was, I am." He lived before Abraham was born, for He was the ever-present, Eternal God.

Hebrews i. 2 says: "his Son, by [through] whom also he made the worlds." If He made the worlds He must have lived before He was born.

He Himself said in John xvi. 28–30 that He had come from God and was going back to God. That statement was so clear, so definite, that His disciples were completely convinced.

Then in John xvii. 5 He prays, "glorify thou me . . . with the glory which I had with thee before the world was." How plain! See John vi. 62. He remembered the distant past. Before the creation of the world He enjoyed and shared in the glory of the Triune God. So He existed before He was born. Thence He was not man but God. ("Always existed" is Phillips' translation in 1 John.)

There is one passage in God's Word that must forever settle the question of the deity and the pre-existence of

Christ. It is found in 2 Corinthians viii. 9, and it is absolutely unanswerable: "For ye know the grace of our Lord Jesus Christ, that, though he *was rich*, yet for our sakes he became poor."

Now let me ask you the question: When was He rich? That He became poor we are all agreed, but the Bible says He was rich. When? I ask. It could not have been after His ascension, for it says He became poor *after* He was rich. In other words, He was rich *first*, then poor. Of course it was before He was born, during His pre-existence, for He always lived and He was always God. He became poor only at His birth. Before His incarnation He was rich.

Colossians i. 17 says: "He is before all things." He was there before anything else was. Again His pre-existence.

(2) *His Omniscience*

He knew all things—past, present and future, where He came from and where He was going, His appointed hour, how He would suffer and die, and when He would rise again. See John xvi. 32.

Matthew ix. 4 says: "Jesus knowing their thoughts." Man cannot read thoughts; only God can do that. See Matthew xii. 25: "Jesus knew their thoughts." Also see John ii. 24-5.

In Matthew xvi. 21 He gives the most minute details regarding His death and predicts His resurrection. Can man describe the manner and place of his death? Of course not. Only God knows the end from the beginning; hence Jesus was God. See also Matthew xvii. 22-3; xvi. 21, Mark x. 33-4, John vi. 34.

In Matthew xxiv. 2 He predicts in detail the destruction of the Temple, and so it came to pass. Can man point to this building or that and foretell what will happen to it?

Jesus did. Then in verse 30 He describes His own return, and that in great detail. He knew.

He says in Matthew xxvi. 13 that an apparently insignificant instance in His life, the anointing in Bethany by Mary, would be preserved, remembered and proclaimed to the entire world. It was. Hundreds of other events have never been recorded—this one was. How did He know?

Another trivial incident is mentioned in Matthew xxvi. 34. He says here that Peter would deny Him and that a rooster would crow. What amazing foreknowledge. Could any man tell what another would do just before the crowing of a cock? Impossible. Jesus was Omniscient.

In Mark xiv. 13 He tells His disciples that they would meet a man with a pitcher of water. An impossible prediction for a mere man, but not for God, who knows the future and exactly what is happening at a given moment. As a matter of fact men did not carry water on their heads in pitchers in the East. That work was performed by women, but Jesus knew that there would be an exception, and that a man would be seen with a pitcher of water on his head.

In John i. 45–51 He sees Nathaniel under a fig tree when no one else sees him, when Nathaniel knew he was completely hidden and when He Himself was nowhere near. There is but one explanation—He was God.

In John iv. 18–29 He tells a perfect stranger the most secret experiences of her life. No wonder she was convinced.

"Lazarus is dead," He said (John xi. 14). How did He know? He wasn't there. No one had informed Him. The disciples had no knowledge of his death. Yet He knew. How? Who was He? Man or God?

(3) *His Character*

"I have sinned in that I have betrayed the innocent blood" (Matt. xxvii. 4), exclaimed Judas, His betrayer. Judas, who knew Him, pronounced Him innocent.

"I find in him no fault at all" (John xviii. 38). That was Pilate's verdict.

"This man has done nothing amiss" (Luke xxiii. 41), cried the dying thief as he hung on the cross.

"Which of you convinceth me of sin" (John viii. 46), challenged Jesus, and no one accepted the challenge.

"In him is no sin" (1 John iii. 5). "Who knew no sin" (2 Cor. v. 21). "Who did no sin" (1 Pet. ii. 22). "Without sin" (Heb. iv. 15). This is the verdict of the Word of God.

Hence, in spite of all the attacks upon Him, His character remains spotless to this day. Jesus was absolutely sinless. His character proves His diety.

(4) *His Teachings*

He spoke with authority, He Himself being the fountain of truth. "Never man spake like this man," exclaimed those who heard Him. Wherever His teachings have gone other religions have passed away.

> *"What words of grace and truth He speaks*
> *Ne'er heard on earth before;*
> *The burdened sinner hears that voice*
> *And feels his sins no more."*

The chasm between the teachings of Jesus and earth's wisest and best is so great that it can never be bridged.

Jesus was never confused or cornered. During the last week of His ministry the Scribes and Pharisees tried again and again to catch Him in His talk, but they always failed. He had an answer ready. No man could have answered correctly as He did. Any ordinary individual would have become confused and at one point or another he would have been cornered. But not Jesus. He even turned the tables on His enemies so that they dare not ask Him any more questions.

To quote from Weymouth: "When Jesus had concluded this discourse, the crowds were filled with amazement at His teaching, for He had been teaching them as one who had authority, and not as their scribes taught" (Matt. vii. 28–9). His teachings prove His deity.

(5) *His Works*

"The works which the Father has given me to finish, the same works that I do, bear witness of me" (John v. 36).

His miracles were unique. He had control of all the laws of nature. His power was unlimited, and He never failed. He demonstrated His power over nature, disease, demons and death. That includes all.

You remember that He controlled the waves. At one time He spoke to the storm and to the sea, saying, "Be still, lie down", and immediately there was a great calm. No man during all the history of the world has ever been able to control nature. Jesus did.

He controlled disease. At His word diseases fled, lepers were cleansed. No man has ever done that.

He had control over demons. Demons cried out and departed when He bade them. No man has ever had that power.

He controlled death. He raised the young man to life at the gate of Nain. He raised the daughter of Jairus to life. He raised Lazarus to life after he had been dead four days. No man has ever had such power as that. Only Jesus was able to demonstrate such power.

> "He calls the dead to life again,
>   Bids winds and billows cease;
> None other man such works hath done—
>   What manner of man is this?"

(6) *His Influence*

Empires have crumbled before His advance, and nations have been transformed by His power. Countless millions own His sway. With a handful of followers He conquered continents and lifted the standards of the human race as no other ever did.

Hence He must be what He claimed to be—the promised Messiah of the Old Testament prophecies, and none other than the Son of God, incarnate in human flesh.

"Is not this the Christ?" exclaimed the woman of Samaria. "This is indeed the Christ, the Saviour of the world" (John iv. 29, 42), was their answer. May we, too, reach the same glorious conclusion.

How He Proved His Deity

(1) He proved His deity by accepting worship. You will remember that both men and angels fell down before Him to do Him homage. In Hebrews i. 6 angels worshipped Him. In Matthew xiv. 33 and in Matthew ix. 17 men worshipped Him. No man in the Word of God ever accepted worship. But He did, and He never forbade it. Therefore He was God.

(2) He proved His deity by forgiving sins. No man can forgive sin—only God can do that. Look, if you will, at Luke v. 20–4 and also Luke vii. 48. The Pharisees accused Him of blasphemy, and rightly so, for, unless He was God, He could not forgive sin. But, because He was God, He did forgive sin.

(3) He proved His deity by concealing Himself at will, and that, too, is something that no man can do. In Luke iv. 30 He suddenly disappeared just when His enemies were sure that they had Him. Again and again He escaped when He was within their grasp, because His

hour had not yet come, and thus, concealing Himself, passed through their midst. He did it because He was God. Man cannot disappear at will.

(4) He proved His deity by dying at will. See John x. 18. You can't. I can't. You can be murdered and you can commit suicide, but you cannot lie down and die when you want to. Nor can you rise again. Jesus could, and He did. You will remember that, as He hung on the Cross, He dismissed His Spirit. Man cannot dismiss his spirit. Only God can do that. Jesus was able to die when His appointed hour had come. Who was He then, man or God?

And because He was and is God, you and I will have to meet Him one of these days, for He is alive for ever-more. We will meet Him as Saviour or as Judge. Which is it to be? Oh, that you would accept Him now as Saviour and exclaim with Thomas of old, "My Lord and my God."

(5) He proved His deity by His stupendous claims. Not only did He claim to be the Son of God, as we have seen (John x. 36); He also claimed to be the King of the Jews (Luke xxiii. 3), and the fulfilment of Old Testament prophecy (Luke xxiv. 2). Moses and David, He said, wrote about Him (John v. 46). When an ordinary man claims to be king we laugh at him. But we do not laugh at Jesus.

Also, He claimed to have been given the prerogative of all future judgment by God Himself (John v. 22), and to have power to raise the dead of all ages (John v. 25–29), and to be the most powerful personage both in Heaven and on earth (Matt. xxviii. 18).

No man in all the history of the world has ever made such stupendous claims. No mere *man* could. His claims were either true or false. If false, then He was a liar, a deceiver, or a lunatic. If true, then He was what He claimed to be—God (John x. 33).

They called Him God, 'twas Thomas who exclaimed,
"My Lord and God," for Jesus was divine.
Yea, He was born of God and not of man.
He made the worlds, created all that is;
He was the Source, the Author of it all,
And by His pow'r alone it still survives.

They called Him God; He did not start to live
When Mary gave Him birth, He always lived;
His birth was but an incident in life,
For lo, from everlasting He was God.
A few short years He tarried in this world,
And then went back to His eternal home.

They called Him God, then worshipped at His feet,
And He accepted worship, being God;
For in the form of God and not of man,
Nor in the form of angels was He known,
His substance was the same as that of God,
The Mighty God—He lives eternally.

CHAPTER VIII

SLANDER—A DANGEROUS WEAPON

N O CHRISTIAN worker can take up the sword of
slander and escape the consequences. "All they
that take the sword shall perish with the sword"
(Matt. xxvi. 52). So spake Jesus, and history has repeat-
edly borne testimony to the truthfulness of His warning.
Men who have slandered others have either been ruined
by slander themselves or have been judged by God with
death.

It makes no difference whatever, be it borne in mind,
whether the slander is true or false—the result is the same.
Judgment is God's prerogative, not man's. His word is
"Touch not mine anointed, and do my prophets no harm"
(Ps. ciii. 15). The statements made may be absolutely
true, but since no mere man is capable of judging, God's
servants are accountable to Him and to Him alone. And
woe betide the man who dares to set himself up as a judge
and publicly slander his fellow-workers! God will not let
it pass. "No weapon that is formed against thee shall
prosper" (Isa. liv. 17).

I could tell of more than one guilty of the awful sin of
slander who has been judged by death, and in some cases
sudden death. "For they that take the sword shall perish
with the sword." Drastic measures may be used. "Who
art thou that judgest another man's servant? To his own
master he standeth or falleth. . . . But why dost thou
judge thy brother? or why dost thou set at naught thy
brother? for we shall all stand before the judgment seat
of Christ. . . . Let us not therefore judge one another any

more" (Rom. xiv. 4, 10, 13). God help us to hearken. Oh, that we might make that our life resolution! In the face of the words of our Lord how can we do otherwise?

"Judge not, that ye be not judged. For with what judgment ye judge, ye shall be judged; and with what measure ye mete, it shall be measured to you again. And why beholdest thou the mote that is in thy brother's eye, but considereth not the beam that is in thine own eye? Or how wilt thou say to thy brother, Let me pull out the mote out of thine eye; and, behold, a beam is in thine own eye? Thou hypocrite, first cast out the beam out of thine own eye; and then shalt thou see clearly to cast out the mote out of thy brother's eye" (Matt. vii. 1–5).

Remember this, my friend: he who slanders is working with the devil. Satan is a slanderer. He is continually accusing us before God. That is his biggest job and his most destructive work. Oh, my brother, are you going to do the devil's work? Are you letting him use you as one of his slanderers? God help you! What carnality! Oh, what a tragedy! God's child but the devil's agent. God's servant working for the devil. A slanderer, an accuser in the pay of the enemy. What a disgraceful state of affairs! Once more I warn you: "All they that take the sword shall perish with the sword."

"I would rather play with the forked lightning," says Dr. A. B. Simpson, "or take in my hands living wires, with their fiery currents, than speak a reckless word against any servant of Christ, or idly repeat the slanderous darts which thousands of Christians are hurling on others."

"The tongue," says God, "is a fire, a world of iniquity: so is the tongue among our members, that it defileth the whole body, and setteth on fire the course of nature; and it is set on fire of hell . . . the tongue can no man tame;

it is an unruly evil, full of deadly poison" (Jas. iii. 6, 8).
And it is with the tongue that the slanderer does his work.

Now Satan seldom uses carnal Christians to retail
slander. He knows they would not be believed. Generally
he chooses one who is noted for piety and is supposed to
be spiritual; one who is characterized by a sanctimonious
air. That kind of a tool he can use.

The gossiper knows everybody's business. He finds out
all about the most intimate family matters. Whenever you
see him he has something new to tell you about someone.
His mind is filled with the failures and sins of others and
he is constantly referring to them.

He knows no mercy nor forgiveness. His whole attitude
is one of condemnation. That Christ was the Friend of
sinners does not affect him. That the prodigal's father
welcomed his wayward son means nothing to him. That
Jesus came, not for the righteous but for sinners, does not
interest him. To him the church is for the righteous only,
never for sinners. His work is to drive them away. He
has no faith in their repentance. Their sin may have been
committed twenty years ago, but they must never be
restored.

God's Word is very clear regarding the one who has
sinned. In 1 Corinthians v. 1–13 he is ex-communicated
because he has not repented, but in 2 Corinthians ii. 1–11
he is forgiven and restored. We must do the same.

I once knew a man who refused to accept any office in
the church. He attended regularly and served most faith-
fully, but he would not accept responsibility. He left the
pastor and his board to deal with everything.

He never interfered with anyone. Those who sinned
and fell he helped. No one ever heard him gossip. He
spoke well of all and never ill of any. He did not interfere
in the lives of those around him. The stories he heard
went in one ear and out the other. He never passed them

on. Every Sunday he was in his place, enjoying the service, getting blessing for his soul. He did not feel that it was his business to deal with the sins of other Christians. He saw to it that he was right and he left the others in God's hands.

He was a wonderful Christian. Everybody loved him. He was never soiled by the filth around him. He went his own way, lived his own life and was always happy in the Lord. Satan could never get him to do his dirty work. He felt he had enough to do to look after himself.

If only we could all learn to do the same how much better it would be! We do not need to steady the ark. God can take care of His own work. Why be a gossiper? Why slander? It is the self-righteous Pharisee that God detests. To the backslider His hand is ever out.

The slanderer will always be in trouble. There is no one more dangerous. Beware of him. Don't listen to his tales. They are always exaggerated. Make him speak in the presence of the one he accuses or be silent. He cannot prove what he says. Challenge him to meet the one of whom he speaks face to face and he will soon back down.

Beware of the one who wants you to confide in him. He may but seek your wreck and ruin. Confide only in God. Take your failures to Him. Let no man be your judge. Avoid the slanderer. He is a garbage collector and what he collects he must dump. He hears of a brother's fall and he must needs tell it to everyone he meets.

The Bible says, "He that covereth a transgression seeketh love; but he that repeateth a matter separateth very friends" (Prov. xvii. 9). If pastors were to repeat the confessions they have heard what chaos there would be! But they cover, they conceal, they protect the one who has confided in them. Not so the slanderer. He repeats the story, repeats it wherever he goes, for his heart is bitter and filled with malice.

God says, "If a brother be overtaken in a fault, ye which are spiritual restore such a one" (Gal. vi. 1). That the slanderer will never do. He is out not to restore but to condemn. If he can put him out of work by repeating the story of his fall to his employer, he is low enough to do it. He has no thought of obeying God's Word, so he makes no effort to restore him. Oh, how heinous is his sin!

"Where no wood is, there the fire goeth out: so where there is no tale-bearer, the strife ceaseth" (Prov. xxvi. 20). Of course, no story could spread of itself. How God rebukes the tale-bearer! Never will he be able to get right until he goes back to all those to whom he has carried the tale and asks their forgiveness. Only then will God pardon his awful sin.

But, you say, it is true. What of it? God can forgive. Do you know all the motives? But, you say, his sin is vile, unmentionable. What of it? God can forgive. But, you say, he should be driven from the church. No, he should be welcomed to the church. That is where he belongs. If the church turns him down, where will he go? But, you say, he will contaminate others. Leave that with God. But his repentance is not sincere, you say. How do you know—are you God? Can you read his heart? Why not leave him alone and attend to your own business? If you cannot love him, at least you need not condemn him.

Heed now the warning voice of God as recorded in Romans ii. 1, Phillips' translation: "Now if you feel inclined to set yourself up as a judge of those who sin, let me assure you, whoever you are, that you are in no position to do so."

Let it be said of me, after I am dead and gone, that my home was always open to back-sliders and sinners, not to repentant sinners alone, but to all sinners; and not just to ordinary sinners but also to vile sinners. Let it never be said that I passed a sinner by just because he was a hypocrite and had never repented, or because he was not genuine. Let it be said that I always stopped and offered him my hand, that I went out of my way to restore him. Otherwise I myself am a hypocrite and a pharisee and I do not know the meaning of Divine forgiveness. God will surely judge me for my attitude toward those who have fallen, both men and women, whether they deserve my friendship or not.

Brethren, where are we heading? What is to be the outcome of it all? Fifty years from now our work will all be done, for many of us much sooner. The future life will then be ours. What will it mean, I wonder, as we stand together at the Judgment Seat of Christ? How ashamed some of us will be. Will we not be sorry we did not leave the judging of one another to the appointed day? For many whom we condemned on earth will be lauded at the Bema, and many whom we approved on earth will be condemned then.

God help us to live, think, act and speak in the light of eternity! Then, instead of getting our eyes on man and judging him, watching for either his virtues or his failures, we will keep our eyes fixed on the Christ who indwells him, and see no man save Jesus—and Jesus only.

CHAPTER IX

THE MESSAGE OF EASTER

WHEN I was in Ancient Russia I visited the Easter services which are held at midnight in the Greek Orthodox Churches.

As the priests, after a long ceremony in which they march three times around the church in search of the body of Christ, re-enter, they cry out, "Christ is Risen", and the people, bowing in adoration, exclaim, "He is risen, indeed!"

That, in a word, is the Easter message. And it is because of the resurrection that we look forward with hope to the final Easter day when we, too, shall rise.

The reality of Christ's resurrection is easily proved. It rests upon the best attested facts in history.

First of all, we have four separate and independent accounts.

On the surface there are contradictions, but a close-up study reveals the harmony that exists between them all.

Admittedly, they must be true or false. They must have been made up independently or together. There is no alternative.

That they could not have been made up independently is demonstrated by the fact that the harmony is by far too complete. They are too much alike. This could not have been had they been manufactured by individuals who had nothing whatever to do with each other.

On the other hand, there could have been no consultation, no previous agreement or understanding, simply because there are too many apparent contradictions. Had the writers collaborated, they would have seen to it that there were no contradictions. Therefore, they were not made up at all, either independently or in consultation. They are true statements of facts. The resurrection of the Lord Jesus Christ was presented by each one as he himself saw it. Thus they are authentic.

In the second place, a careful study of the resurrection reveals the fact that most of the accounts were written by eye-witnesses. Those who wrote saw with their own eyes the risen Christ.

The story is related simply and with no attempt to colour it or exaggerate. One tells what another omits. This accounts for the apparent contradictions and differences.

Had they made it up years later they would certainly have represented Him as appearing to His enemies and confounding them. That would have been the natural climax to the story. No writer of fiction would have thought of anything else. What an opportunity they missed! But the fact is, He appeared only to His disciples.

In the third place, even infidels admit that His disciples believed He had risen.

Renan, for instance, said that it was a hallucinated woman who gave the world a resurrected God. But that is impossible and absurd, for there was a Matthew and a Thomas to convince and a Paul to convert.

Strauss declares that His appearances were visionary. But the eleven and the five hundred could not have had the same vision.

Others insist that He never died. What, then, of the "water and blood"? How account for it if He were not dead?

Moreover, His enemies guarded His body, and if He had only fainted He would have been weak and would not have been able to escape from the tomb.

Last of all, Jesus Himself would have been an impostor.

He stated that He would rise and He did. After His resurrection He declared that He had risen from the dead. If His word was untrue, then He was a liar and unworthy of our allegiance.

The resurrection of the Lord Jesus Christ is one of the best attested facts in history. There are hundreds of historical events that do not have nearly as many witnesses. Just think, there were fourteen groups that saw Him alive after His death:

1. Mary Magdalene at the tomb.
2. The women.
3. Peter.
4. The two disciples at Emmaus.
5. The disciples in the upper room.
6. The disciples with Thomas.
7. The disciples on the shore of Galilee.
8. The eleven on a mountain.
9. The five hundred brethren at once.
10. James.
11. The disciples on Olivet at the Ascension.
12. Stephen at his martyrdom.
13. Paul on the road to Damascus.
14. John on Patmos.

Now, some of these witnesses saw Him, not once, but several times. How could they have been mistaken?

The fact that many of them died for their testimony shows their reliability. Men do not die for nothing, not voluntarily. Yet these men and women gladly suffered martyrdom rather than deny their Lord.

Had these witnesses been false their enemies would have produced contrary evidence. Whereas, the best thing they could do was to spread the story about the disciples having stolen His body while the soldiers were asleep.

But note, if you will, that that was the soldiers' story. They were asleep, so they said, and while sleeping they saw the disciples come and steal His body. Strange things to see when one is asleep.

And think of a Roman guard being asleep, every man. Impossible!

On the other hand, how are you going to harmonize the theft with the order in which the graveclothes were found, the handkerchief, etc.? When thieves break in they leave everything in confusion. But not so in the tomb of Jesus. The handkerchief was folded neatly and laid in a place by itself. The graveclothes were left in an orderly condition. There were no signs of fright and haste as there would have been had the nervous disciples attempted to take His body from the tomb.

For you must never forget the fear of His followers. They were afraid. In fact, they all forsook Him and fled. They had lost every atom of courage. And hence they would have been the last ones in the world to attempt the theft of a dead body from a tomb surrounded by a Roman guard.

And in any case, how are you going to account for the miraculous change from fear to courage, and even boldness, as a result of His resurrection? Had they stolen His body they would have remained in hiding. But the fact that they came out boldly, openly and publicly and proclaimed His resurrection, even going so far as to accuse the Jews and the members of the Sanhedrin of murdering Him, proves conclusively that they had nothing to do with His reappearance.

No, His enemies produced no contrary evidence. They had nothing to say. Their explanations were childish, absurd and impossible. But had He not risen, how quickly they would have proven it.

The founders of all the world's religions have died, nor

have they ever been resurrected. Christ and Christ alone arose.

When Talleyrand, the great agnostic, wanted to found a new religion, and finding it hard going, asked counsel of the King of France, he received this answer: "Go and be crucified, and on the third day rise again and men will believe in your religion."

> "Up from the grave He arose,
>   With a mighty triumph o'er His foes;
> He arose a Victor from the dark domain,
>   And He lives forever with His saints to reign,
> He arose! He arose! Hallelujah! Christ arose!"

And because Christ rose, we, too, shall rise, for His resurrection is the guarantee of ours.

But, some will ask, with what bodies will we appear? That question was asked and answered by Paul long ago. We shall be like Him, we are told. And if we can discover the kind of body He had we will know something of the body that we too shall have on that Day.

A Spiritual Body

First of all, it is clear from the Word of God that our Lord was given a spiritual body. Then we, too, will have spiritual bodies. And what is a spiritual body? A body that is not subject to natural law.

After our Lord was raised from the dead He could not be kept in or out by gates and bars. When the disciples were gathered together, first without Thomas and then with him, Jesus suddenly appeared in their midst. How He got in no one knew. But there He was. And as He ate before them and showed them His hands and His side, they knew that it was Jesus Himself, and that in spite of the fact that the doors were shut He came in.

So will it be with us. Walls will form no barrier. We will be able to pass through them as easily as we now pass through the air we breathe. Gravitation will no longer be able to hold us. To step off a high building will be perfectly safe. Without laboriously climbing stairs we will be able to ascend of our own free will.

Space will be annihilated. We will be able to go from place to place unhindered and unhampered, and at any speed we choose. Distance will mean nothing. If we desire to speed from planet to planet it will be easy, for we shall have spiritual bodies, and a spiritual body is not subject to natural law.

A Powerful Body

In the second place, our Lord was given a powerful body. And we, too, shall have powerful bodies. Today we grow tired and weary. Oft-times we are unable to complete our tasks, or to do the work that we long to do. We become weary and exhausted. We have to rest. Sleep is necessary. Sometimes a long vacation is inevitable, and all because these bodies of ours wear out.

But with our resurrection body we will never know fatigue. Never again will we say, "I am tired." All weariness will be gone. Our bodies will never become exhausted. Sleep will not be necessary. Never again will we be compelled to stop and rest. With our resurrection bodies we will have all the endurance necessary for our work. How wonderful it will be never to be weary again.

An Immortal Body

Then, too, our Lord had an immortal body, a body that could never die. And we, too, shall have such a body. There can be no death in heaven. The Bible tells us that the last enemy that shall be destroyed is death. And what an enemy it has been! It takes our friends from us, breaks up our families, separates husband and wife, child and parent. It sends the undertaker to our home and provides a casket for our loved ones. It brings the tears to our eyes and leaves us with an ache in our hearts. It peoples our cemeteries and spreads its blight on every side.

Such an enemy is death. But in that Day there will be no death. Never again will we have to die. There will be no funerals in Heaven, no crêpe on the doors. Cemeteries will be unknown. The work of the undertaker will be over. Never again will there be a separation. Death will be no more. Immortal bodies cannot die.

An Incorruptible Body

But again, our Lord had an incorruptible body. And our resurrection bodies will also be incorruptible. Every seven years these bodies of ours undergo a change. They have to be renewed from time to time. They are continually corrupting. But in the resurrection life corruption will be unknown. Our bodies will last forever. There will be no decay, no corruption. Corruption belongs to earth. We shall have incorruptible bodies.

A Glorified Body

Lastly, our Lord was given a glorified body, a body so glorious that it outshone the glory of the sun. And we, too, shall have glorified bodies, bodies infinitely brighter than the noon-day sun.

We are given a glimpse of such a body on the Mount of Transfiguration, where, it is said, the very raiment of our Lord glistened and shone as He was transfigured in the presence of His disciples. Thus will we shine through all eternity.

They that turn many to righteousness, says God, shall shine as the stars for ever and ever. The brightest sun ever created will look dim in contrast to the brightness of our glorified bodies. Light unapproachable by human beings will be ours. So glorious will our bodies be that the very angels will look at us in wonder and amazement.

Like Him

How beautiful we will be in that day it is impossible to say. All we know is that we are told that we will be like Him. He died when He was about thirty-three years of age. Hence He will be eternally young. Wrinkles, therefore, will be gone and the beauty of youth, glorified by the resurrection, restored.

We shall be changed, we are told, changed into His likeness, and with those who have gone before, caught up to meet the Lord in the air. And, oh, what a change! It is to this we look forward as we celebrate another Easter.

And when will it take place? When are we to receive our resurrection bodies? When are all these promises to be fulfilled? At the time of the Second Coming of our Lord. It will be when He returns. No one until then will be resurrected. Today God's people await that morn. The trumpet shall sound. The dead in Christ will be raised, living believers changed, and both caught up to meet the Lord in the air.

Then will come the Bema judgment, the day of rewards, and the marriage supper of the Lamb; after that our reign with Christ for a thousand years, and then, endless eternity.

Oh, what a prospect! No wonder we glory in Easter. Not only does it remind us of the resurrection of our Lord, but, as already stated, it speaks to us of our own resurrection and the glories that await. Glad Easter Day!

CHAPTER X

"BEHOLD, I have given him for a witness to the people, a leader and commander to the people" (Isa. lv. 4).

God's plan is that His flock should be led by a Shepherd, not run by a board. Committees are to advise, never to dictate. The Holy Spirit appoints men. To bishops and elders is given the care of the churches, never to committees. They are to be the overseers, the shepherds. Each one has his own flock. Because men have failed to recognize this, there has been trouble. When God's plan is followed, all is well.

"The Seven", generally designated "deacons", had no voice in the management of the church at all. They were chosen for the one and only purpose of distributing the daily food in an equal and orderly way, and for no other. It was their business to serve the tables.

The Bible knows of no other plan. All down the centuries it has been the same. When God wanted something done He chose a *man*, equipped and fitted him for the task, placed him at the head of His people and told them to follow and obey. Thus arose the prophets, great mighty leaders who, having caught the vision, imparted it to others and carried out God's purpose. Never did He select a committee; never did He choose a board. He called and commissioned *men*.

Almost all Bible history gathers around men, their birth and Call, their work, their lives, the successes and failures, the things they did and taught, and, finally, their death. Biography holds a large place in the sacred Record.

Think, if you will, of Abraham, of Jacob and of Joseph. God wants a nation and He chooses Abraham. He wants a saviour and He chooses Joseph, not a committee. And in the days of famine Egypt has a one-man government. He wants a deliverer and He takes Moses. He might have gone to the elders of Israel and selected a board. He did not. His call is to one man. To him He gives the vision, and Moses becomes God's representative, the great leader of His people.

Moses dies. Who now is to carry on? Do the people get together and choose a committee to guide them into the Promised Land? By no means. God sends them another leader. Joshua is anointed for the task (Num. xxvii. 15–23). Later they get into difficulty. What now do they do? Form a committee? Not at all. They cry to God for a deliverer. They know God's plan. They must have a leader, one man, to whom they can look. God answers and Samson is sent. And through all that dark, dark period God's plan operates. Judge after judge is sent, until at last Samuel, the greatest of them all, becomes their leader.

The years go by. Another shepherd is needed. God tells Samuel to anoint David. Samuel dies, dies and leaves, not a committee, but a shepherd boy. Thus David, God's anointed, becomes the Shepherd of Israel. And years later, when the nation has backslidden, Elijah appears and other great prophets, kings and reformers, who turn the people back to God.

In the New Testament era it is the same. First, John the Baptist, then Jesus, God's only begotten Son. Now comes the launching of the Church. How is it to be done? By a board? No. By men filled with the Holy Ghost. Peter goes to the Jews and Paul to the Gentiles. And so the task is accomplished.

Next, the mighty reformers, Luther, Calvin, Knox and others, heralds of the Reformation. Again there is work to do, and revivalists are needed. Wesley is chosen and with him Whitefield. Later Finney, Spurgeon, Moody, etc. Foreign fields are to be reached and Carey, Judson, Livingstone and Taylor hear the Call, see the vision and go. And if boards were formed and committees chosen, it was after, not before. It was because God's man, hearing, obeyed and imparted the vision to others. And the committees were formed, not to control and command, mark you, not to dictate, but to help and co-operate, to assist their God-chosen leaders.

But what is to be done when the leader dies? Must not the committee carry on? Yes, but how? Ah, here is where the mistake is made! It is now that the most subtle of all dangers appears. The first temptation is to take the work out of the leader's hands while he is still alive, to begin to dictate. That is always disastrous. Destruction is certain to follow such an innovation. The leader must hold his God-given place at the head. Advice he will welcome, co-operation and help he will need, but dictation he must reject. The flesh covets power. Hence boards, if led by the flesh, will assume, more and more, a tone of authority, until at last they will become utterly unworkable. The Holy Ghost will be grieved, the glory depart and the work cease.

But when the leader dies, what then? Well, what then? Has God another plan? Does His policy change? By no means. The committee will be tempted to take over all power and authority and seek to carry on. But sooner or later the work will fall into decay, the vision pass away, and the committee dissolve. What then is the committee to do? Choose another leader. Get down before God and cry for a divinely chosen successor. Seek God's man, the man with God's vision for the work. God will have him ready. There is always an Elisha upon whom the mantle of Elijah will fall.

And when he appears, follow him. Give to him the same loyal support and co-operation as to the founder. Seek his vision. Get his viewpoint. Accept his plans. If he is wise, he will want the counsel of his brethren, he will welcome the advice of his committee. Therefore, instead of dictating, assist. For if he is God's man he will have God's vision; and even though his plans and methods may be utterly different, they will be eminently successful. To hold back and question, to block and thwart, to oppose and criticize is to invite disaster.

The committee or board that dares to take over the management instead of choosing God's divinely appointed leader will find their time largely occupied with questions of law and order, and their efforts blocked by self-made constitutional restrictions, until they are burdened beyond measure with the necessity of making endless amendments in order that their actions may be legalized. When such a condition obtains and the days are thus spent it is high time to scrap the constitution.

The danger of expending untold energy on mere words and phrases in which no one apart from those deeply versed in the legal side of things ever offers a suggestion, and the placing of numerous motions on the books that pertain so often to small non-essentials, is to starve and stultify the entire movement. Where glowing reports of advancement, problems in connection with the task, ways and means of prosecuting the work, and prayer for God's guidance and blessing—in a word, where the spiritual is emphasized, there is blessing. But when the spiritual is made subservient to the technical and legal, there is bound to be dissatisfaction and terrible disappointment. A return to God's plan is the only remedy.

The most successful kind of management is that of

appointment and dismissal. There isn't a business firm in the world that could carry on under any other system. If a man is eligible for the position he receives an appointment. If he fails to make good, he is dismissed. It was thus at the beginning. Paul ordained or appointed elders in every church. Any other order is not only unscriptural but unworkable.

If a business firm were to govern itself as churches do, it would go bankrupt in no time. Think of the president of a large company choosing a committee to assist and advise him in the management of the business. Think of him giving the committee power to legislate, vote and decide important issues. Think of him being compelled to abide by the decision of the majority even when he knew the policy adopted would spell utter ruin. And then think of that committee, failing to get his vision, opposed to his policy, finally voting him out altogether, robbing him, as it were, of his own child, and taking over the management themselves. I wonder how many weeks or months it would take them to totally wreck the great business enterprise which he had spent long years building up?

I am thinking now of just such tragedies in the religious world, and there are many of them. A pastor prays, toils and travails until at last he gives birth to a God-imparted vision. Of his own free will he invites a number of men to associate themselves with him in the care of this child, dearer to him than life itself. But they disagree with his policy even though the child for which he has sacrificed everything is in a flourishing condition; and finally, through their lack of appreciation and vision, they force him to abandon his offspring, thinking they in their blindness know better how to care for it.

He goes, his soul wrung with anguish, his heart torn and bleeding. He appeals to those higher up, but in vain. They compromise with the usurpers, ignore what he has done, and let him suffer on. The men whom he was kind enough to invite, in whom he trusted, now take charge. The child grows weaker and weaker. Common sense would tell them to send in desperation for the father to save it, but no, they prefer to watch its death struggles as it gasps for life, knowing not that they have wrought its ruin. Oh, when will we awaken! God help us to get the vision!

If a leader is worthy of the position, he is worthy to be followed. If he cannot be trusted, he ought not to be the leader. The man who is qualified to be the pastor of a congregation is entitled to the loyal allegiance and support of every member of his flock. If the official board feel that they must run the church and that he must take his orders and get his vision from them, then they ought not to have him as their pastor at all. If a man is capable of being the pastor, he is capable of leading the flock and guiding the church.

I know of a certain church, founded by a leader divinely chosen and commissioned, that prospered exceedingly as long as God's order was followed. The committee caught the vision and followed to a man. Crowds gathered, souls were saved, and believers edified. Money flowed in until all debts were paid and thousands of dollars sent to the foreign field. The devil attacked from the outside in every conceivable way and failed. Finally he struck from within. First one man began to question and oppose God's chosen leader, the pastor of the work. The seed thus sown took root in the heart of another, who at first compromised, then completely sided with the other.

Gradually the opposition deepened and spread, until at last the leader, whom every one freely admitted was God's man in God's place, rather than fight those who had missed the plan of the Holy Ghost and commenced first to dictate, then to oppose, resigned. But that was the end of peace, blessing and prosperity. They had touched God's anointed. The crowds disappeared, souls no longer sought the enquiry rooms, division and strife characterized the meetings of the committee, and finally the glory departed. Oh, what a catastrophe! And all because a committee, failing to recognize the Holy Ghost, began to dictate instead of follow.

Strange to say, there seemed to be no repentance, that is, on the part of those responsible. They watched the crowds decrease and the money fail. They saw the thronging multitudes scattered all over the city, absorbed by other works. The time came when there were only a handful attending. The enquiry rooms were no longer filled with souls seeking Christ. Yet they made no effort to get God's chosen leader back, even though he was still available. Even though he had humbled himself many times and had freely offered to do all in his power to save the work. Ah, no, there was no penitence, no humility on the part of those who had touched the ark and wrecked everything.

They first called another man, thinking it made no difference who came so long as he was capable. But he was not God's choice and before long he left. Then they turned to another, this time the best they could find, and in him they built their hopes. Surely, they thought, he will succeed. But they were still blind to God's plan. The crowds disappeared like snow before the sun. Troubles of all kinds arose, and at last, he, too, had to leave. Whereas, had they been willing to humble themselves and restore the work to its rightful leader it would have flourished and prospered at once.

Of course, God blessed His leader, blessed him abundantly in other fields, even though He could not bless the work that had been kept from him. For several years he waited, waited in sorrow and anguish of heart, broken,

humbled, crushed. Waited, thinking continually that the
usurpers would come to their senses at last and right the
wrong. But in vain. And finally God led him into other
work and did more for him than ever before. It seemed
at first that he had lost all. His own beloved child had
been taken. But in reality he gained all. For their loss
was his gain, whereas his gain might have been theirs as
well.

It was because of this that Korah and his company
perished. They became jealous, you remember, and
objected to the God-ordained leadership of Moses and
Aaron. "Ye take too much upon you. Wherefore lift ye
up yourselves above the congregation of the Lord?" Thus
they argued. There were two hundred and fifty of them,
and they thought they should be a committee to guide
the destinies of Israel, and in Moses' answer he makes it
plain that by murmuring against him and against Aaron
they had "gathered together against the Lord".

Serious, is it not? "Touch not mine anointed, and do
my prophets no harm," is God's command. How did it
end? Why, the way it always ends. In judgment, terrible,
awful beyond description. The earth opened, and with
their wives and children, their flocks and herds, their
tents and all that was theirs, they went down alive, and
the earth closed over them until they were sealed in death.
It pays to let God's leaders lead (Num. xvi).

Well do I remember a great leader with whom it was
my privilege at one time to labour. He had on his board
men with very little vision, and they endeavoured to
harness him. He must work in the old rut; he must obey
the letter of the law and adhere strictly to the constitution.
He stood it as long as he could, and at last, after they
had wrecked him in health, and burdened him until he
could bear no more, he went away and died of a broken
heart. Nor has the work ever prospered since.

Oh, my brethren, if God favours you by giving one of His chosen and anointed servants, a true leader, follow him. Give him rein; and when you cannot understand, trust. God has him in hand and God will lead him through.

If he is a real leader, remember, he will make mistakes. The man who never makes mistakes never does anything. I would rather make a hundred mistakes and accomplish something than to make no mistakes and accomplish nothing. Mistakes are not sins. Man always has and always will err. God allows him to blunder again and again in order to teach him and keep him humble.

Give me a leader who blunders but gets somewhere rather than one who stays in the old rut, never makes a mistake nor anything else. I know a man whose blunders are legion. That same man, because he is a man of God, because his heart is right, and because he has God's vision, in the midst of his mistakes and in spite of blunders, is doing things for the Kingdom that not one of his critics would ever dare attempt. God can use such a man.

When a war breaks out men are sent into battle, not under a committee but under a general. In the great world war of 1914–18 it became necessary to unite the forces under the command of one man, Foch. The disagreement of a committee on the field of battle, and the delay necessitated by voting would have lost the day. Every nation recognizes that. When a vessel puts out to sea it is placed under the command of a captain, and his word is supreme. No ship would dream of sailing with a committee in charge. The word of one man is law. And so it is in every crisis situation. The power must be held by one man. To get things done requires a head. And a true leader, worthy of responsibility, will accomplish what no board in the world could ever hope to do. Why then try to attempt, in the spiritual realm, that which cannot be done in the natural? Verily, the children of this world are wiser than the children of light.

God's ideal government, remember, is a theocracy, an absolute monarchy, with Jesus Christ as the Monarch. The devil also has the same plan. He will before long produce the Antichrist, the superman, a dictator, the world's leader. And, mark you, it will be the strongest government ever set up. Later, God will send Jesus to reign as King of kings. To Him no committee will dare dictate, nor will He bow to any board. No, not even a committee of angels and archangels with Gabriel as chairman. His word will be law. That is how God will get things done, and that is His chosen plan in human leadership, even now.

Leadership is priceless. Money cannot compensate for the services rendered. Despise it not, therefore, but accept it as from God. It is His plan. He has no other. It is yours to follow, for where God gives a leader He always gives others to be led. When he sends a shepherd He always has a flock to be shepherded. One man must lead, many follow. And, as your leader follows Christ, you follow him, for God's plan is that His flock should be led by a shepherd, not run by a board. Committees are to advise, never to dictate. The Holy Spirit anoints men.

"Behold, I have given him for a witness to the people, a leader and a commander to the people" (Isa. lv. 4).

CHAPTER XI

CAN ORGANIZED RELIGION SURVIVE?

THERE are three great branches of the Christian Church: the Greek Orthodox, the Roman Catholic, and the Protestant. In France, Church and State have been separated and Roman Catholicism excluded from politics. In Russia the same thing has happened; the Greek Orthodox Church has been wounded unto death. The question, therefore, arises: Will Protestantism, likewise, be judged in America and England? Or, *can Organized Religion survive?*

My question is not, "Can *Religion* survive?" To that enquiry I would have to answer "Yes". For man is a religious being, no matter where you find him. Even the atheism of Russia is but another form of religion. It is the satanic expression of man's religious instincts. Hence *Religion* will survive. But this is my question: "Can *Organized* Religion survive?" And to that I answer without hesitation, "No!" *Organized* Religion cannot survive. It will be overthrown.

All apostate Christianity is doomed. And I base my contention on the seventeenth chapter of Revelation. The Scarlet Woman, representing, as she does, the various apostate religious systems of the last days, after triumphing both religiously and politically, is at last left desolate and naked, the flesh of her outward show eaten, and she herself burnt with fire. Such is to be the ultimate doom of all religious systems, both Catholic and Protestant.

But why? Well, let me answer that question by asking another: "*Do the religious systems of today represent the*

Christianity of Jesus Christ?" And first we will hear from
God's Word:

"Wherewith shall I come before the Lord, and bow
myself before the high God? shall I come before Him with
burnt offerings, with calves of a year old? Will the Lord
be pleased with thousands of rams, or with ten thousands
of rivers of oil? shall I give my first-born for my transgression, the fruit of my body for the sin of my soul?
He hath showed thee, O man, what is good; and what
doth the Lord require of thee, but to do justly, and
to love mercy, and to walk humbly with thy God?"
(Mic. vi. 6–8).

"I hate, I despise your feast days, and I will not smell
in your solemn assemblies. Though ye offer me burnt
offerings and your meat offerings, I will not accept them;
neither will I regard the peace offerings of your fat beasts.
Take thou away from me the noise of thy songs; for I
will not hear the melody of thy viols. But let judgment
run down as waters, and righteousness as a mighty
stream" (Amos v. 21–4).

"To what purpose is the multitude of your sacrifices
unto me? saith the Lord: I am full of the burnt offerings
of rams, and the fat of fed beasts; and I delight not in the
blood of bullocks, or of lambs, or of he-goats. When ye
come to appear before me, who hath required this at your
hand, to tread my courts? Bring no more vain oblations;
incense is an abomination unto me; the new moons and
sabbaths, the calling of assemblies, I cannot away with;
it is iniquity, even the solemn meeting. Your new moons
and your appointed feasts my soul hateth: they are a
trouble unto me; I am weary to bear them. And when
ye spread forth your hands, I will hide mine eyes from
you: yea, when ye make many prayers, I will not hear:
your hands are full of blood. Wash you, make you clean;
put away the evil of your doings from before mine eyes;

cease to do evil; learn to do well; seek judgment, relieve the oppressed, judge the fatherless, plead for the widow" (Isa. i. 11–17).

Read these verses again, carefully, thoughtfully, prayerfully, and my question *"Do the religious systems of today represent the Christianity of Jesus Christ?"* will be answered.

Now please do not infer that I am classing all alike, or think that I am finding fault with various local churches simply because they belong to some religious denomination. I am not. By no means. There are thousands of churches the world over that are absolutely true to the Word of God and evangelical truth and practice. Multitudes of ministers there are who preach the old-fashioned Gospel and seek to win souls to Jesus Christ. Christians of all denominations are to be found who are living godly lives in this present evil world. They pray, they love the Bible, they are deeply spiritual, and loyal to God. All this I know and gladly admit. Of such churches and Christians I do not speak, regardless of their denominational affiliation. My contention has to do with the religious systems as a whole, the great outward display of so-called Christianity, that which was likened by Christ to a mustard tree, in which birds, both good and bad, lodged.

Religion is not Salvation. Religion is of man's "doing"; Salvation is of God's providing. Religion is Godward; Salvation is manward. Religion is do and don't, form and ceremony, creed and doctrine, rites and rituals; Salvation is life. Religion is what man gives to God; Salvation is what God gives to man. Religion is of works; Salvation is of grace. Religion is man made; hence every tribe and nation has its own peculiar religious practices. Religion has its fasts and prayers; its feasts and festivals; its vestments and robes, its rules and regulations. Religion exalts man; Salvation honours God.

Now "religion", mere outward "religion", God hates, every form of it. "I hate, I despise your feast days," He says.

Could language be stronger? What a wholesale condemnation of religion! Again, I say, God hates religion. Religion crucified His Son. Religion has burnt His martyrs at the stake. Religion has persecuted His followers all down the centuries. Religion is oftentimes a curse. But Salvation is a blessing. Paul could not be saved through what he called "the Jew's religion". Judaism cannot save. If it could, Christ would never have died. Christianity cannot save, neither Catholic, Protestant, nor Greek Orthodox. Not religion, not the church, but *Christ,* a Person. In Him is life. "He that hath the Son hath life; and he that hath not the Son of God hath not life" (1 John v. 12). Religion is not Salvation. Christianity is not religion; Christianity is Christ.

The religious systems of today—what are they? From whom do they derive their authority? Were they founded by Jesus Christ, or do they date back to some man or group of men? Are their various doctrines and practices to be found in the New Testament? Have they divine authority? Or are they all man-made, man-invented, and man-given? In other words, do they come from the Councils of the Church, or the Church Fathers, and therefore from man, or do they come from God?

I am afraid, very much afraid, that after a candid investigation it will be found that they came, many of them, from the Council of Trent, the Council of Lateran, the Council of Florence, the so-called Church Fathers, and the pronouncements of fallible popes, etc.; but from the Word of God, never. Hence, they are without divine authority, and are, therefore, in no wise binding.

For my authority I appeal directly to Jesus Christ. His scathing denunciation of the Pharisees for their adherence to man-made traditions and commandments in place of the Word of God is unparalleled in Scripture. And how any religious body can deliberately ignore His words and still cling to purely human inventions and innovations is beyond all understanding. Here are His words, the words of Jesus Christ Himself, in answer to the question put to Him by the Pharisees. Hear Him:

"Why walk not thy disciples according to *the tradition of the elders,* but eat bread with unwashen hands?" inquired the Pharisees. Mark, in explaining the situation, tells how the Pharisees had found fault with Him because His disciples had not washed. "For the Pharisees, and all the Jews," he explains, "except they wash their hands oft, eat not, holding *the tradition of the elders.*" And thus answered Jesus: "Well hath Esaias prophesied of you hypocrites, as it is written, This people honoureth me with their lips, but their heart is far from me. Howbeit in vain do they worship me, teaching for doctrines *the commandments of men.* For laying aside *the commandment of God,* ye hold *the tradition of men.* Full well ye reject *the commandment of God,* that ye may keep *your own tradition,* making *the Word of God* of none effect through *your tradition,* which ye have delivered: and many such like things do ye" (Mark vii. 1–13).

And yet there are those who still hold to "tradition" in preference to the Word of God, when it only is authoritative.

My friends, much as I regret it, I am bound to answer "No" to my question: "Do the religious systems of today represent the Christianity of Jesus Christ?" They certainly do not. The early disciples would never recognize them, for they are no more like New Testament Christianity than Protestantism is like Roman Catholicism.

It was because of this that Bolshevism throttled Christianity almost to death in Russia. Mummies of so-called saints, which had been worshipped by millions and by means of which the priests made a fat living, were dragged out and broken open to prove that they were nothing more than bundles of rags and papers. No wonder the people lost faith in the Greek Orthodox religion. Who wouldn't? Such deliberate deception deserves no mercy.

I saw with my own eyes, when I was over there, so-called relics of dead men's bones, the bones of the saints, pieces of the cross, etc. What rubbish! And to think that intelligent people believe in them. Talk about the superstition of the Dark Ages, and the idolatry of paganism— it would be hard to imagine anything so abominable. I don't wonder that Bolshevism did what it did. It was not Christianity that it demolished, but a false system of Christianity unknown in the New Testament Scriptures.

Christianity, true Christianity, can never be destroyed by Bolshevism or any other power. It has nothing that can be destroyed. Christianity is Life, Eternal Life, and Life is indestructible. Buildings can be burned, cathedrals razed, bells melted, ikons broken, schools and colleges levelled to the ground, but Life!—Life can never be destroyed. The body may be killed, martyrs burned at the stake, and meetings forbidden, but Life, God-Life in the heart of man, cannot be annihilated. "The blood of the martyrs is the seed of the Church."

Religion can be overthrown, and false systems of Christianity destroyed. That is why the Church has been all but annihilated in Russia. It was outward pomp and show.

Do not think that I am in any way justifying Bolshevism. By no means. God used Assyria as His axe with which to hew His people Israel. He used Babylon to punish Judah. He used the Philistines and other Gentile nations during the days of the Judges because of the sins of His people. He used them, but afterwards He always punished the axe, the nation He had used. They never once escaped. Nor will Bolshevism. Its day of judgment is coming just as surely as it was God's axe in Russia. And terrible indeed will be the judgment meted out.

Bolshevism did not need to cruelly murder in cold blood some three million people. The atrocities committed can never be excused. Bolshevism will reap as it sowed, and what a harvest! God help it when the judgment falls! It will not go unpunished. Bolshevism has repeated the sins of the Tsars a hundredfold. Tens of thousands have been sent into exile, without cause. Multitudes have been cruelly butchered. Horrible crimes have been perpetrated by the Communists in Russia, deeds that belong to the Stone Age or the most savage paganism. But God is still on His throne, and His day will come.

"Why do the heathen rage, and the people imagine a vain thing? The kings of the earth set themselves, and the rulers take counsel together, against the Lord, and against his Anointed, saying: Let us break their bands asunder, and cast away their cords from us. He that sitteth in the heavens shall laugh: the Lord shall have them in derision. Then shall He speak unto them in His wrath, and vex them in His sore displeasure" (Ps. ii. 1–5).

But, finally, organized religion cannot survive because it lacks the one great essential of Christianity, namely, *love*. There is but little of love in the religious systems of the day, and love characterized all that Jesus did. It was the heart of His message and the motive of His work. He came to reveal the Father's love, a love so great "that he gave his only begotten Son". "Love is of God." "God is love." "Now abideth faith, hope, love, these three; but the greatest of these is love."

But what do we find in organized religion? Instead of love, hate. Between the various State Churches strife and division.

Religion has burnt men at the stake, not pagans, but other religious men. Religion has stoned the prophets, sawn them asunder, driven them to the dens and caves of the earth, crucified and beheaded them, tortured them in cold, dark dungeons, sent them into Siberian exile, slain them in bloody pogroms, stretched them on the rack, flogged them to death—in a word, persecuted them with all the hatred of the most savage heart.

Religion massacred the Huguenots and the Waldensians; it drove the Stundists to the mines of Siberia, cruelly murdered the Jews, and through the Spanish Inquisition instigated the most hellish deeds ever perpetrated. Religion has done all this and more. Religion has murdered its millions. I say it has hated, not loved, for had it been characterized by love these atrocities of hate could never have been committed.

But, thank God, we know that no sooner will organized religion be overthrown, and a world ruler take over the governments of earth, than the Golden Age will be ushered in, with Jesus Christ reigning as Lord of lords and King of kings, in glorious, millennial power and splendour, earth's last great potentate destroyed, and the kingdoms of this world become the kingdoms of our Lord and of His Christ. Then, at last, Christianity, true Christianity, will flourish, for all corrupt forms of Christianity, man's religion, will have been destroyed.